'Earley and Jones have focused their insightful and substantive attention on a topic that is highly relevant to both a UK and an international audience. Although the issue of the lengthy period of time to headship is less of a problem in other national contexts, the topic of accelerated leadership development is no less problematic. Because leading schools has become intense and complex and the need for leaders to quickly turn around schools is now a major national policy agenda in the U.S., rigorous and relevant information on the models and approaches of accelerated leadership development is critical. The authors have provided both a theoretical and practical perspective that informs policy, contributes to quality professional development and sets directions for future research.'

**Gary M. Crow, Professor of Educational Leadership and
Policy Studies, Indiana University, USA**

'This is the first major book to focus on accelerated leadership development, a phenomenon of great contemporary significance, because of the succession challenges facing many developed countries. Peter Earley and Jeff Jones should be congratulated on bringing together the research and literature on this important theme in such a clear and accessible manner. Policy-makers and senior practitioners will find much of value in this book, as they consider how to develop new school leaders.'

Tony Bush, Professor of Educational Leadership, University of Warwick, UK

'How can we tackle the impending leadership crisis in schools? With nearly a quarter of headteachers due to retire in the next five years, we need to replace the *ad hoc* arrangements of the past with a systematic approach to leadership recruitment. This invaluable book by Peter Earley and Jeff Jones shows the way. Accelerated leadership development is a highly controversial issue, often generating more heat than light. Now, in this concise volume, we have an essential comprehensive guide which combines rigorous exploration of the concept, detailed examples from the public and private sector, cogent analysis of two major national education programmes and a practical strategy that schools can follow. When I read a book like this I ask the fundamental question – can I use and apply it in my work? The answer is a resounding 'Yes!'. Leadership talent spotting must be seen by schools, consortia and local authorities as a priority. This book gives them the means of doing this which is both professionally credible and practically compelling.'

**Graham Handscomb, Senior Manager, Essex County Council;
Fellow of the Chartered Management Institute, UK**

'Peter Earley and Jeff Jones have provided a very timely volume to support schools in their quest to identify, develop and support potential future senior leaders and headteachers. At this time of a potential future shortage of senior leaders and headteachers, this book provides schools with the tools to ensure that they can successfully develop tomorrow's senior leaders so they are able to lead teaching and learning for the benefit of all young people in the future. All schools will benefit from the strategies offered in this book – ignore at your peril!'

**Robin Newman, Deputy Headteacher, Notley High School &
Braintree Sixth Form, UK; MBA in Educational Leadership participant
at the Institute of Education, University of London**

'This publication fills a niche that is evident in schools (and other educational institutions) internationally. Building upon relevant theory and practice of school leadership, it interrogates accelerated leadership development through many lenses. It therefore has interest and significance for both existing leaders looking to the future of their institution as well as to aspiring leaders striving to understand their potential career choices. The authors provide springboards for contextual analysis and for the development of leaders to meet each institution's unique needs. It is a book of wide professional appeal.'

Jackie Walkington, Director, National Centre for Research on Professional Experience and Teaching (NCR PET), Faculty of Education, University of Canberra, Australia

'There is no more important task facing our schools system than the development of school leaders, particularly for challenging schools where their impact is essential in closing the achievement gap. This book provides a wide-ranging and thorough examination of the theory and practice of accelerated leadership development both in schools and in the wider public and private sectors – for those of us involved in designing and delivering such programmes, it's a "must-have".'

Heath Monk, Chief Executive Officer, Future Leaders

Accelerated Leadership Development

The Bedford Way Papers Series

22 *Teaching in Further Education: New perspectives for a changing context*
Norman Lucas

23 *Legalised Leadership: Law-based educational reform in England and what it does to school leadership and headteachers*
Dan Gibton

24 *Theorising Quality in Higher Education*
Louise Morley

25 *Music Psychology in Education*
Susan Hallam

26 *Policy-making and Policy Learning in 14–19 Education*
Edited by David Raffe and Ken Spours

27 *New Designs for Teachers' Professional Learning*
Edited by Jon Pickering, Caroline Daly and Norbert Pachler

28 *The Dearing Report: Ten years on*
Edited by David Watson and Michael Amoah

29 *History, Politics and Policy-making in Education: A festschrift presented to Richard Aldrich*
Edited by David Crook and Gary McCulloch

30 *Public Sector Reform: Principles for improving the education system*
Frank Coffield, Richard Steer, Rebecca Allen, Anna Vignoles, Gemma Moss and Carol Vincent

31 *Educational Resource Management: An international perspective*
Derek Glover and Rosamund Levačić

32 *Education in a Global City: Essays from London*
Edited by Tim Brighouse and Leisha Fullick

33 *Exploring Professionalism*
Edited by Bryan Cunningham

34 *Music Education in the 21st Century in the United Kingdom: Achievements, analysis and aspirations*
Edited by Susan Hallam and Andrea Creech

35 *Critical Practice in Teacher Education: A study of professional learning*
Edited by Ruth Heilbronn and John Yandell

A full list of Bedford Way Papers, including earlier books in the series, can be requested by emailing ioepublications@ioe.ac.uk

Accelerated Leadership Development
Fast tracking school leaders

Peter Earley and Jeff Jones

Institute of Education, University of London
Bedford Way Papers

First published in 2010 by the Institute of Education,
University of London, 20 Bedford Way, London WC1H 0AL

www.ioe.ac.uk/publications

© Institute of Education, University of London 2011

British Library Cataloguing in Publication Data:
A catalogue record for this publication is available from the
British Library

ISBN 978 0 85473 884 7

Typeset by Quadrant Infotech (India) Pvt Ltd
Printed by Cats Solutions

Contents

List of figures and tables   viii

List of abbreviations   ix

Preface   x

Acknowledgements   xii

1   Introduction: Why accelerated leadership development and why now?   1

PART 1 APPROACHES TO ACCELERATED LEADERSHIP DEVELOPMENT

2   Accelerated leadership development: Theory and concepts   14

3   Accelerated leadership development: Approaches and methods   28

4   High potential programmes: Examples from the private and public sectors   35

PART 2 ACCELERATED LEADERSHIP DEVELOPMENT IN SCHOOLS

5   Accelerating the development of school staff   44

6   Accelerated leadership development in schools: Fast-track teachers   55

7   Accelerated leadership development in schools: Future Leaders   65

8   A fast-track leadership development strategy for schools   75

9   The challenge of fast tracking   86

10 Conclusion   93

References   97

Index   106

Figures and tables

Figures

1.1   A model of leadership development

8.1   Leadership development survey

Tables

2.1   Strategic perspectives on talent management

2.2   Strategic choices at different phases of the TM process

2.3   Framework of different strategic perspectives through which organisations deploy talent management

2.4   Eighteen dimensions that affect the operational impact of talent management

2.5   Potential organisational and individual derailers

3.1   Selection of fast-track participants – three examples

3.2   Developmental experiences

4.1   Characteristics of talent management schemes in all sectors

4.2   Leadership development methods

5.1   Key trends in leadership development programmes

5.2   Developmental experiences with impact

5.3   Greenhouse Schools – developing potential

6.1   Examples of Fast Track training options

7.1   Destination posts of Future Leader cohorts 1 and 2 at the end of their one-year residency

8.1   General and psychological characteristics displayed by talented staff

Abbreviations

ALD   Accelerated leadership development

ASCL   Association of School and College Leaders

CMI   Chartered Management Institute

CPD   Continuing professional development

DCSF   Department for Children, Schools and Families

DfES   Department for Education and Skills

FL   Future Leaders

HR   Human resources

LAs   Local authorities

NAHT   National Association of Head Teachers

NCSL   National College for School Leadership

NCLSCS   National College for Leadership of Schools and Children's Services (also referred to as 'The National College' or 'the College')

NLNS   New Leaders for New Schools

NLP   Neuro-linguistic programming

NPQH   National Professional Qualification for Headship

QTS   Qualified teacher status

SLT   Senior leadership team

SQH   Scottish Qualification for Headship

TDA   Training and Development Agency for Schools

TLR   Teaching and learning responsibility

TM   Talent management

Preface

This book, which is designed to be of interest to both academics and practitioners, focuses on issues surrounding accelerating the leadership development of staff in schools in England and elsewhere. The growing interest in accelerated leadership development is largely a result of the large number of headteachers and other senior staff in schools due to retire or leave the profession prematurely. Already there are problems in identifying suitably experienced candidates to appoint to such posts. An added complexity is the negative perception that some middle and senior leaders have about headship, which is discouraging them from applying for such posts. Furthermore, the time it currently takes to become a headteacher – 'heading for the top' takes about 20 years to achieve in England – is regarded by some aspirants to the role as a hindrance to their career progression. Therefore, policy-makers need to find ways of making the job more attractive and speeding up the development of potential leaders so that they will have the necessary motivation, skills and confidence to take on senior leadership positions.

With the benefit of funding from the (then) National College for School Leadership[1] we have been able to investigate leadership development practices in education, as well as in private and public sector organisations in the UK and elsewhere. Some organisations have long and successful experience of running schemes for accelerating the leadership development of their staff. This book is intended to capture and communicate the main lessons learned from this work to help schools address the leadership succession planning and talent management issues they currently face. Can fast tracking school leaders work and, if so, how?

Accelerating leadership is not simply a matter of acquiring factual knowledge about how to lead in a school setting. Personal learning from experience is an essential element in acquiring practical skills such as leadership. For most professions, it takes considerable time to learn from a variety of experiences to become a fully competent professional. This book is concerned with how to speed up the process of developing leaders in schools by planning and assisting their learning from experience and from formal learning opportunities.

The book is especially relevant to those responsible for leadership development in education and those who wish to learn how to lead and manage in schools. It will be of interest to those concerned with accelerating leadership development in all school contexts and, as such, will appeal to an international as well as a national readership. The book's emphasis on both theoretical and practical perspectives enables it to be used as a specialist text for use on postgraduate courses and for both academics and practitioners. It consists of two parts: Part 1 investigates approaches to accelerated leadership development, while the focus of Part 2 is on the education sector and the mechanisms that have been used to help develop leaders and realise potential of talented staff. We hope you will find it an interesting and useful read.

Professor Peter Earley and Dr Jeff Jones

Note

1   From September 2009, in recognition of its wider remit, the NCSL was renamed as the National College for Leadership of Schools and Children's Services.

Acknowledgements

The authors would like to thank all who have contributed in some way to this publication. Particular thanks are due to the National College for funding the literature review, Dr Geraldine Hutchinson and Richard Churches from CfBT for their contribution to Chapter 6 and to Sara Bubb for her editing.

We would also like to thank Taylor & Francis for permission to publish extracts from *School Leadership and Management* (Vol. 29, No. 3, 2009), a special issue on 'approaches to leadership development' edited by the authors.

We are indebted to a large number of organisations and their staff for being prepared to discuss their approaches to accelerated leadership development. We would like to remind readers that the details of organisational schemes described in the book may have altered since the data were gathered.

The authors and publisher gratefully acknowledge the permission granted to reproduce copyright material in this book.

Excerpts from the following publications were reprinted with permission of the National College for Leadership of Schools and Children's Services. These are also marked in the text: *Leadership Succession: An overview* (2007); *Leadership Succession – A framework for action* (2008); *What are we learning about…identifying talent?* (Evidence in Practice Guide) (2009); *Greenhouse Schools: Lessons from schools that grow their own leaders* (2006).

Excerpt from the following reprinted with permission of John Wiley & Sons, Inc.: Gritzmacher, P., 'Strategic management of fast-track employees', *National Productivity Review* (Vol. 8, No. 4, 1989), pp. 421–32. Copyright ©1989, John Wiley & Sons.

Tables 3.2 and 5.2 reprinted with permission from *People & Strategy (Journal of HRPS)*, 1998 12-1. Copyright 2010. All rights reserved.

Tables 2.3, 2.4 and 4.1 reprinted with permission from Chartered Management Institute and Ashridge Consulting: *Talent Management: Maximising talent for business performance* (2007) London: Chartered Management Institute and Ashridge Consulting.

Table 2.2 reprinted with permission from Ashridge Consulting: Lubitsh, G. and Smith, I. (Spring 2007) 'Talent management: a strategic imperative' in *360° The Ashridge Journal*, p. 9.

Excerpt from the following reprinted with permission of Stanford Educational Leadership Institute: Davis, S., Darling-Hammond, L., LaPointe, M. and Meyerson, D. (2005) *School Leadership Study: Developing successful principals*, Stanford Educational Leadership Institute.

Table 5.1 reprinted with permission from Mel West and David Jackson: West, M. and Jackson, D. (2002), 'Developing School Leaders: A comparative study of school preparation programmes', paper presented at *AERA Annual Conference*, New Orleans, April.

Extract reproduced by permission of SAGE Publications, London, Los Angeles, New Delhi and Singapore, from Fink, D. (2010) *The Succession Challenge: Building and sustaining leadership capacity through succession management.* Copyright (© SAGE, 2010).

Every effort has been made to trace copyright holders and to obtain their permission for the use of copyright material. The publisher apologises for any errors or omissions in the above list and would be grateful if notified of any corrections that should be incorporated in future reprints or editions of this book.

Chapter 1

Introduction: Why accelerated leadership development and why now?

- **What is leadership development?**
- **The emergence of accelerated leadership development**
- **The picture of headteacher recruitment**
- **The need for succession planning and talent management**
- **The succession challenge and a framework for action**

For some time now it has been widely acknowledged that high-quality leadership is one of the key requirements of successful schools (e.g. Bush and Jackson, 2002; Davies, 2009) and that leaders can have a significant positive impact on student outcomes (Day *et al.*, 2009; Matthews, 2009; O'Donoghue and Clarke, 2010; Pont *et al.*, 2008; Robinson *et al.*, 2008). The key role of effective leaders, particularly headteachers, is emphasised, for example, in a report from the National Audit Office (2006: 9). This focused on improving poorly performing schools and stated that 'without an effective headteacher, a school is unlikely to have a culture of high expectations, or strive for continuous improvement'. More recently the (then) Department for Children, Schools and Families (DCSF, 2008) used inspection data to show that for every 100 schools in England that have 'good' leadership and management, 93 will have 'good' standards of achievement, but for every 100 that do not, only one school will have good standards of achievement. Not a single example was found of a school 'turning round' its performance in the absence of good leadership.

The discourse of leadership is in the ascendancy and the range of popular and academic literature on leadership has become extensive (e.g. Adair, 2003; Charan *et al.*, 2001; Collins, 2001; Goleman *et al.*, 2002; Taylor, 2002). In the last 60 years or so there has been substantial interest and research into what effective leadership looks like, with as many as 65 different classification systems developed to define the field (Fleishman *et al.*, 1991) and over 300 definitions of leadership (Bush and Glover, 2003). Northouse

(2004), in a comprehensive review of the leadership literature, notes the wide variety of theoretical perspectives (e.g. Bryman, 1992; Gardner, 1990; Hickman, 1998; Rost, 1990) and points to the fundamental differences between trait, behaviourist, political and humanistic approaches or theories. He points to the emerging view that leadership is a process which can be observed in the behaviours of leaders (Jago, 1982) and the need for leaders and followers to be understood in relation to one another (Hollander, 1992) and as a collective whole (Burns, 1978). Northouse (2004: 3) synthesises this continuum in a single definition of leadership – 'a process whereby an individual influences a group of individuals to achieve a common goal'.

With reference to the education sector, Earley and Weindling (2004) note the changing discourse of the relevant literature – from an emphasis on management to one of leadership – and provide a useful overview of the literature, referring to a wide research base to outline the main features of effective educational leadership. Several typologies are offered and leadership theory is categorised chronologically under five headings: trait, style, contingency, influence, and personal trait theory. The latter characterises effective leadership as superior individual performance. Earley and Weindling see the dominant conceptions of leadership in education currently as being transformational, learning-centred and distributed. A strong literature on educational leadership is now in place (Day *et al.,* 2009; Leithwood *et al.,* 2006a) and synergies and read-across to other research fields are becoming increasingly common (Day *et al.,* 2010; Jones, 2005; Leithwood *et al.,* 2006b). The literature on leadership development and how to grow and develop leaders, including educational leaders, is also expanding.

What is leadership development?

We begin this chapter by briefly considering the broad concept of leadership development. According to Bolden (2005: 3), 'the issue of leadership development and its impact remains highly contentious'. He goes on to emphasise that, 'central to the argument about the effectiveness of leadership development is the question of whether or not you can train or develop leaders'. It is our contention that you can develop and train people to take on leadership roles, but is there a need to identify those who are perceived to have 'leadership potential' and who will therefore benefit from such attention? As will be shown, there are many who argue that we should identify talent early and concentrate resources on their development.

Day (2001: 582) defines leadership development succinctly as 'expanding the collective capacity of organizational members to engage effectively in leadership roles and processes', while Bolam (2003: 75), writing about the education sector, proposes that leadership development is:

an ongoing process of education, training, learning and support activities taking place in either external or work-based settings proactively engaged in by qualified, professional teachers, headteachers and other school leaders aimed primarily at promoting the learning and development of professionally appropriate knowledge, skills and values to help school leaders to decide on and implement valued changes in their leadership and management behaviour so that they can promote high quality education for their students more effectively thus achieving an agreed balance between individual, school and national needs.

Leadership development refers to the activities involved in strengthening one's ability to establish clear vision and achievable goals and to motivate others to subscribe to the same vision and goals. Leadership development is critical at almost *any* level in an organisation – not just the executive or senior level. Importantly, leadership development is an ongoing process and can take place in both external or work-based settings.

In drawing a distinction between the terms 'management' and 'leadership' development, Day (2001: 582) proposes that the latter is 'orientated towards building capacity in anticipation of unforeseen challenges'. Because of its concern with the growth of collective organisational capacity, he also regards leadership development as a process involving each person within the organisation. Commenting on the usefulness of Day's distinction above, Bolden (2007) proposes another distinction, that between 'leader development' and 'leadership development'. He regards the former as 'an investment in human capital to enhance intrapersonal competence for selected individuals' (Bolden, 2007: 5), whereas the latter is 'an investment in social capital to develop interpersonal networks and cooperation within organisations and other social systems'.

As a recent review of leadership development by Bush notes:

Much of the research suggests that leadership development should go beyond leader development, through programmes and other interventions, to a wider focus on the school as an organisation. It is concerned with the ways in which attitudes are fostered, action empowered, and the learning organisation stimulated.

(Bush, 2008: 42)

He goes on to state that the term 'leadership development' is widely used, but notes that:

most NCSL programmes are targeted at individuals and may more accurately be regarded as 'leader development'. While preparing middle and senior leaders is important, it seems evident that the wider issue of leadership development for school improvement has been under-represented by the College. Team programmes provide for groups of staff and the evaluations suggest that, where schools provide fertile learning environments, gains can be powerful... multiple participation provides extra school-wide benefits.

(Bush, 2008: 87)

Lumby *et al.* (2004) offer a conceptual model that is particularly helpful when considering leadership development. This model has two axes: the horizontal 'leadership' continuum from the individual to the collective; and the vertical 'leadership development' axis with a continuum from the prescribed (skills and competencies) to the emergent (leadership as a bundle of qualities). If these two are superimposed, the quadrants emerge (see Figure 1.1).

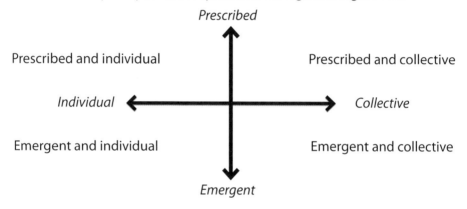

Figure 1.1: A model of leadership development

Source: Lumby *et al.*, 2004.

However it is defined, leadership development was often considered to be part of an off-site programme or course away from the workplace. The best programmes try to combine both on-site and off-site experiences and benefit from the strengths of both workplace and workshop learning.

The emergence of accelerated leadership development

In this extensive body of writing and research, leadership development, succession planning and talent management are now increasingly seen as key strategic priorities. In the business world, the level of challenge has been contrasted to a war (Michaels *et al.*, 2001; Tulgan, 2001). Regardless of economic conditions, business can ill afford to lose its best people to its competitors or fail to develop its people to the full. In its publication, *What we know about school leadership* (NCSL, 2007a), the (then) National College for School Leadership (NCSL) does not specifically refer to warfare but does make reference to the demographic 'time-bomb' which, it argues, needs defusing. Part of the answer to the challenge of filling headship vacancies which, as we show later, continues to be a major problem, is to question the time it takes to become a head. This, it is argued, is too long and the system requires 'more leaders than current approaches to promoting staff are presently able to produce' (NCSL, 2007a: 15). 'Heading for the top' needs to be a shorter journey, but those achieving senior leadership posts need to be as well qualified and at least as able to lead as those arriving by more traditional and lengthier routes.

The demographic challenge is compounded by 'negative perceptions of the work and the role of school leaders – especially regarding accountabilities and workload' (NCSL, 2008a: 15). Thus, to 'go into battle' or address this 'crisis' in recruitment, England's National College advised ministers that there needed to be more fast tracking in schools of those with leadership potential. This means:

> *early identification of talent, and mentoring and coaching these individuals; and providing them with many opportunities to lead – in their own and other schools – to broaden their knowledge of school contexts and types and to increase the number of headteacher role models they can draw on.*
>
> (NCSL, 2008a: 15)

It is against this policy backcloth that consideration has been given in the education sector recently to fast-track and accelerated leadership development programmes, in the belief that they can successfully respond to the recruitment challenge by producing high-quality candidates for headship. In other sectors, as will be shown, the practice for the identification and development of 'talent' varies, with the actual succession planning processes employed suited to the context of the particular sector or business.

The picture of headteacher recruitment

Howson (2006) issued a reminder that 10–12 per cent of the 23,000 schools in England advertise for a headteacher each year. In secondary schools, this figure (440) is some 75 (or about 20 per cent) more than ten years ago. In 2005/06, over 2,600 primary and secondary schools advertised for a new headteacher. Around a quarter of secondary schools and a third of primary schools failed to make an appointment (NCSL, 2007b). According to the NCSL (2007b: 3), almost one-third of primary and secondary headships are re-advertised because no suitable candidate comes forward.

Nearly a quarter of headteachers are aged over 55, and as they retire over the next five years, the profession is deprived of a great swathe of experienced leaders. At the same time, too few candidates are putting themselves forward for the role.

Because of the growing international concern, a study was commissioned by the Scottish Government to make recommendations about the recruitment and retention of headteachers in Scotland. The authors of the report (MacBeath *et al.*, 2009) found the following:

- Of the 336 headship vacancies during the period of the study, 117 were re-advertised one or more times.
- Twenty-two per cent of male heads and 24 per cent of females would not recommend headship to anyone. Overall, more than half (53 per cent) said they would not urge others to go for the top job, or were not sure.
- The chief reasons were the long hours and the demands of accountability to inspectors and local authorities. The majority of heads said they worked for more than 50 hours a week, with 45 per cent spending up to 65 hours on school-related tasks.
- Several hurdles stood in the way to headship – for example the demanding nature of qualifications such as the Scottish Qualification for Headship (SQH), which could be difficult to fit around work and family commitments. Almost three-quarters of teachers (73 per cent) said they had no intention of pursuing the official route to leadership.
- However challenging and stressful, 88 per cent still perceived headship to be a privilege and offered a valued opportunity to make a difference to children's learning.

Hargreaves and Fink (2006) emphasise the need to replace the *ad hoc* approach of the past with a systematic approach to leadership recruitment and development. They believe that this is a key means to tackling the impending shortage of headteachers. In England, it is generally accepted that responding to the succession challenge will require a multi-agency approach. To underline the complexity of this challenge, the NCSL (2007b) refers to several inter-related challenges at work, including the retirement boom, perceptions of headship, length of apprenticeships and regional variations:

- *The retirement boom* – The implications of a potential recruitment crisis surrounding future school leaders have already been noted. The fact that too few new leaders are emerging as replacements leaves policy-makers with a complex problem: how to increase the number of school leaders coming through by around 15–20 per cent over the next two or three years.
- *Perceptions of headship* – The demands made upon school leaders have grown exponentially over recent years and, as a consequence, few would dispute that the role of the headteacher is a challenging one. NCSL (2007c) found that, while 43 per cent of deputies say they had no desire to move up the ladder, nine out of ten heads found the job rewarding.

- *Extended 'apprenticeship'* – Traditionally, the time it takes to become a headteacher is considerable, often taking the best part of 20 years. Several commentators have observed that it tends to take longer to gain a headship than it does to achieve a comparable level of seniority in many other professions. The challenge for policy-makers is to reduce the time it takes to become a headteacher, thereby accelerating the development process.
- *National and regional variations* – In a survey commissioned by the National Association of Head Teachers (NAHT) and the Association of School and College Leaders (ASCL), Howson (2006) found quite significant variations in the success experienced by schools in their attempts to appoint new headteachers.

The last point is reinforced by Thomson (2009), who argues that, while the paucity of applicants for headship posts is an international phenomenon, it is not universal. She draws on a wide body of international literature to show that the shortages tend to be in particular locations (e.g. inner-city, rural); types of school (e.g. high schools in challenging circumstances and serving disadvantaged children, Catholic schools); and sizes of schools (e.g. small primary schools). She also points to the reluctance of serving heads to stay to retirement age, although attitudes to this may change in the light of economic circumstances.

The picture of headteacher recruitment has also to be considered alongside the issue of the quality of applicants. In their study of key issues in developing school leaders in the USA, Davis *et al.* (2005) identified five inter-related factors that, in various ways, affected the supply of good applicants for headships and their quality. They note the following:

- The role of principal has expanded to include an array of professional tasks and competencies, causing many to argue that the job requirements far exceed what is reasonable. The demands of the job have changed so much that traditional methods of preparing administrators are no longer adequate to meet the leadership challenges posed by schools.
- School districts are struggling to attract and retain an adequate supply of highly qualified candidates for leadership roles.
- Principal candidates and existing principals are often ill-prepared and inadequately supported to organise schools to improve learning while managing all the other demands of the job.
- School districts reported a shortage of highly qualified principal candidates with almost 60 per cent of principals planning to retire, resign or otherwise leave their positions during the next five years. In parts of the country, the issue focused more on the dwindling

supply than on the inequitable distribution of qualified candidates in suburban and affluent communities. For example, the problem in California is not a shortage of certified administrators (school leaders), but one of highly qualified administrators committed to working in underserved communities and schools.

- Despite the principal shortage, an increasing number of school leaders are being certified. It appears that the processes and standards by which many principal preparation programmes traditionally screen, select and graduate candidates are often ill-defined, irregularly applied, and lacking in rigour. According to the National Policy Board for Educational Administrators (2001), this has resulted in many aspiring administrators being admitted too easily and passed through the system on the basis of their academic work rather than on a comprehensive assessment of the knowledge, skills and dispositions needed to successfully lead schools.

Leadership preparation, succession planning and leadership development clearly represent major policy challenges to government and school boards/ governing bodies alike, and not only in England.

The need for succession planning and talent management

The key to any succession planning process is the identification and management of talent. Leading public organisations have recognised that a more strategic approach to managing people, and in particular succession planning, including managing high-potential staff, is essential to fill key vacancies and for change initiatives to transform their cultures. For example, in the USA, the General Accounting Office (GAO) investigated how agencies in Australia, Canada, New Zealand and the UK were adopting a more strategic approach to managing succession of senior executives and other public sector employees with critical skills. Their report stated that:

> leading organisations engage in broad, integrated succession planning and management efforts that focus on strengthening both current and future organisational capacity. As part of this approach, these organisations identify, develop, and select successors who are the right people, with the right skills, at the right time for leadership and other key positions.
>
> (GAO, 2003: 1)

Collectively, these agencies' succession planning and talent management initiatives demonstrated the following six practices:

1. They receive the active support and commitment of the organisation's top leadership;
2. There was close integration with the organisation's strategic plans;
3. They emphasise developmental assignments in addition to formal thinking;
4. They address specific human capital challenges such as diversity, leadership capacity and retention;
5. They facilitate broader transformation efforts;
6. They identify talent from multiple organisational levels, early in careers, or with critical skills.

Regarding the last point, both private and public sector organisations face an increasingly complex and ever-changing landscape in their attempts to acquire, retain, motivate and develop the talent needed to keep their businesses operating effectively and competitively. According to McCartney and Garrow (2006: 12) organisations have been forced to focus on talent management because:

> The trend for restructuring and business downsizing has eroded much emerging leadership talent. Shrinking 25–45 year old demographics and the swell of leaders now approaching mandatory retirement age decreases the talent pool available to organisations dramatically. Competition for talent is fierce with companies who are willing and able to offer more attractive packages and perks.

Many organisations within the UK, both public and private, operate programmes for the development and advancement of employees who are recognised as having potential. In the literature, staff demonstrating high potential are usually seen as the top 20 per cent of staff, but in practice the term usually relates to those in the top 2–5 per cent of staff. In the public sector, high-potential programmes have traditionally operated within the Civil Service, local government, the police, fire service, and the health service. McCartney and Garrow (2006) concluded that organisations see talent management as a means of:

- securing future growth and sustainability;
- reducing turnover and retaining top talent;
- streamlining the business;
- enabling high performance.

Organisations and sectors, including education, ignore these issues at their peril. In England, the National College has led a major initiative to address the issues around succession planning so as to be in a strong position locally to develop the school leaders of tomorrow.

The succession challenge and a framework for action

As the National College states, succession planning in education should be a systematic, and not an *ad hoc*, approach to leadership recruitment and development. This, it claims, is crucial to addressing the impending shortage of headteachers (NCSL, 2007c) and ensuring that emerging leaders 'are of high quality and equipped with the skills necessary for modern headship' (NCSL, 2009b: 84). Over the last few years the leadership succession and succession planning strategy of the National College, which was established in 2007, has been extensive and based on local rather than national solutions. It has resulted in a wealth of practical materials being produced for schools and local authorities (LAs) to use when considering their own solutions (National College, 2010). Their website offers a wide range of materials [www.nationalcollege.org.uk/], some of which are noted in later chapters and in the references.

Summary

To develop people and to avoid a potential shortage of school leaders in the future, leadership talent development must be seen by all schools and their leaders as a priority. Many writers have focused on this and see it as a responsibility of leaders to develop the next generation of teachers. For example, Fullan (2008), Collins (2001) and others have asked whether there is a pool of high-quality leaders who will be able to take over when leaders depart. Succession planning is about legacy and the main focus of this book – accelerated leadership development – is a central part of that planning process.

The remainder of this book consists of two parts and a concluding chapter. Part 1 investigates approaches to accelerated leadership development, drawing predominantly upon what we know from research and experiences outside the education sector. Chapter 2 draws upon relevant literature to outline the main theories and concepts underlying accelerated leadership development, while Chapter 3 looks at the approaches and methods for developing leaders. The final chapter (Chapter 4) in Part 1 gives brief examples from the private and public sectors of leadership development programmes for staff deemed to display high potential.

The focus of Part 2 is on accelerated leadership development in the education sector and it begins Chapter 5 with an account of mechanisms that have been used in schools to help develop leaders and realise the potential of talented staff. Chapters 6 and 7 draw upon the authors' experiences of being involved in two national accelerated leadership development programmes – the Fast Track teachers and Future Leaders schemes. Chapter 8 is more practical in orientation and it proposes 'six considerations' or a model for schools that helps them develop support structures and systems to make the right choices when developing leaders. The concluding chapters attempt to bring together the main themes of the book, highlighting some of the unresolved and controversial issues underpinning attempts to fast track teachers to senior leadership positions.

PART 1

APPROACHES TO ACCELERATED LEADERSHIP DEVELOPMENT

Accelerated leadership development: Theory and concepts

- **Accelerated leadership development (ALD) and its attendant concepts**
- **The extent of ALD programmes**
- **Characteristics of high-potential and fast-track staff**
- **Role of line managers**

This chapter provides a synthesis of the theory that underpins the accelerated development of managers and leaders. The role of the line manager within the development of high-performing employees is critical in accelerating and sustaining development, and research suggests that the most compelling development occurs in the workplace, rather than through courses or other formal training. The role of those people involved in the daily management and support of high-potential staff is therefore critical and deserves particular attention. The extent of ALD programmes and the characteristics of high-potential and fast-track staff are also described, but we commence with a discussion of key terms and concepts so we can begin to make sense of what is a rather complex field.

Accelerated leadership development and its attendant concepts

This section considers the many concepts associated with accelerated development such as talent management, acceleration pools, and high potential. A variety of similar and inter-related terms about accelerated leadership development and fast tracking are found in the literature; this section attempts to clarify their respective meanings.

Succession planning

Over time, succession planning has shifted its focus away from being a reactive process of job replacement to a more proactive one that takes a longer-term view. Leibman *et al.* (1996: 16) define succession planning as:

> the deliberate and systematic effort made by an organisation to identify, develop, and retain individuals with a range of leadership competencies who are capable of implementing current and future organisational goals.

Succession planning is complex and is part of a succession management process where:

> one or more successors are identified for key posts (or groups of similar key posts) and career moves and/or development activities planned for these successors.
>
> (Hirsch, 2000: 10).

The focus of succession planning tends to be only on the most senior staff, such as the chief executive officer or managing director. The literature suggests that succession planning needs to be aligned with other areas of people management (Human Resource Management), including talent management, learning and development processes, and performance management and pay reviews.

Talent management

There are many definitions of talent management. For example, the Chartered Institute of Personnel and Development (CIPD) see talent management as:

> the systematic attraction, identification, development, engagement/ retention and deployment of those individuals with high potential who are of particular value to the organisation.
>
> (CIPD, 2006: 1)

Talent management involves having formal processes in place to recruit, develop and retain the organisation's 'best' people. As the National College notes:

> The heart of talent management lies in spotting leadership potential and connecting it with the key leadership roles. Formal and objective assessment, often using feedback and diagnostic tools, can indicate readiness to move in the short term as well as long-term potential.
>
> (NCSL, 2008a: 127)

The delineation between succession planning and talent management is not always clear. *The War for Talent* report (Michaels *et al.,* 2001), produced by the McKinsey Corporation in the late 1990s, showed that the concept of talent management has evolved into a common management practice, and what was once solely attached to recruitment now covers a multitude of areas including organisational capability, individual development, performance enhancement, and succession planning (McCartney and Garrow, 2006).

Both succession planning and talent management are dynamic processes occurring in changing times. An absence of alignment can cause difficulties, such as having a transparent talent management process and a secretive succession planning process. In turn, talent management can be an effective 'feeder' process for succession planning, sometimes incorporating succession planning altogether within its leadership and management processes.

Blass (2007: 3) defines talent management as 'the additional management processes and opportunities that are made available to people in the organisation who are considered to be "talent"'. Her observations are that different organisations are seeking to achieve different things from their talent management systems. This reflects the various strategic perspectives available to organisations, as outlined in Table 2.1.

Table 2.1: Strategic perspectives on talent management

Strategic perspective	Shapes the way in which the talent management system is viewed, implemented, and put into operation.
Process perspective	Proposes that it includes all processes needed to optimise people within an organisation.
Cultural perspective	Believes that talent management is a mindset and that it is needed for success.
Competitive perspective	Is underpinned by the belief that talent management is about identifying talented people, finding out what they want, and giving it to them – if not, competitors will.
Developmental perspective	Proposes that talent management is about accelerated development paths for the highest potential employees.
Human resources (HR) planning perspective	Claims that talent management is about having the right people matched to the right jobs at the right time, and doing the right things.
Change management perspective	Uses the talent management process to drive change.

Lubitsh and Smith (2007) found that a talent management system is specific to each organisation and must be designed to take account of a unique blend of strategy, people, culture and systems. Their research enabled them to identify a framework of 13 dimensions that present various strategic choices at different phases of the talent management (TM) process (see Table 2.2).

Table 2.2: Strategic choices at different phases of the TM process

Strategic consideration	Dimensions	Operational considerations
Why talent?	1 Risk	How much risk is the organisation prepared to tolerate in its decisions around career and succession planning? To what extent does our response relate to our organisational culture?
	2 Transparency	How transparent is the system in the organisation? To what extent are our talented people informed and involved in talent management?
	3 Culture	How competitive is the organisation's culture?
Definition and entry point	4 Decision process	How broad is the group of people that decides who is talent?
	5 Permanency of definition	How permanent is the classification of 'talent'?
	6 Size of talent pool	How many people are included in the talent pool?
	7 Ease of entry	How easy is it to enter the talent pool?
Managing the talent	8 Ownership of talent	Where is the ownership of talent viewed to be in the organisation?
	9 Connected conversations	How many people are having connected conversations with individuals about their careers?
	10 Development path	How are people developed once they have been identified as talent?

	11 Development focus	Where does the focus of the organisation's development activities lie?
	12 Support	How much support is provided to the talent pool?
Outcomes and benefits	13 Performance management	How is people's performance measured in the organisation?

Source: adapted from Lubitsh and Smith, 2007.

Acceleration pools

Byham *et al.* (2002) propose a different approach to grooming future leaders and executive talent: acceleration pools. Rather than targeting one or two hand-picked people for each executive position, an acceleration pool develops a group of high-potential candidates for executive jobs in general. The development of these pool members is accelerated through 'stretch' jobs and task-force assignments that offer the best learning and highest visibility opportunities. Those in the pool are assigned a mentor, receive more training, and participate in special developmental experiences, e.g. executive programmes and action learning sessions. In addition to receiving more feedback and coaching, pool members are tracked by senior management and checked for their development and readiness for advancement. A comprehensive process for setting up and running an acceleration pool is outlined in *Leadership Succession: A framework for action* (NCSL, 2008b: 86–7). It notes four distinct aspects: Establish; Populate; Develop; and Evaluate:

1. Establish
   - Define potential for senior leadership or rapid progression
   - Agree your offer to participants: development portfolio, incentives
   - Determine scale and scope, and allocate resources
   - Assign project manager.
2. Populate
   - Spot potential leaders during talent identification process
   - Issue invitation
   - Induct participants.
3. Develop (repeated in an ongoing cycle)
   - Assess individual strengths and weaknesses
   - Create individual development plans
   - Evaluate risk and plan mitigation
   - Assign personal mentors
   - Establish a participant network
   - Place in new roles as appropriate.

4. Evaluate
   - Track individual progress
   - Seek feedback from participants
   - Evaluate the effectiveness of development activities.

Assessment for acceleration pools needs to be rigorous for them to gain a reputation for high quality. The selection process and the criteria for assessment must be transparent and fair – not privileging certain categories or types of employee. Any scheme must adhere to equal opportunities and be non-discriminatory on any grounds other than 'role performance'. For success, entrants must feel proud of being invited to join and organisations should place an additional value on people emerging from the pool.

High potentials

The term 'high potentials' is used to denote individuals who are perceived to be likely future organisational leaders. High-potential performers, sometimes referred to as 'HIPPOs', are identified in a number of ways, as is shown later.

Leadership pipeline

Some organisations have regularly utilised systematic approaches to filling leadership positions. This planned process has sought to forecast leadership requirements, identify a pool of high-potential candidates, develop the leadership competencies of this pool through intentional learning experiences, and then select leaders from the larger pool of potential leaders. The aim of this planned and systematic process is to create a 'leadership pipeline' that supplies the organisation's future talent needs. According to Hartle and Thomas (2003: 6), 'the leadership pipeline model is based on the principle that there is a hierarchy of work which gets more complex as the individual works up through the organisation'.

Because of the many different terms deployed and because organisations have problems in finding a clear definition of talent management, research carried out jointly by the Chartered Management Institute (CMI) and Ashridge Consulting (2007) set out to provide a broad definition of talent management, a framework to help understand the different strategic perspectives through which organisations deploy talent management (see Table 2.3) and a range of 18 dimensions that affect the operational impact of talent management (see Table 2.4).

Table 2.3: Framework of different strategic perspectives through which organisations deploy talent management

Perspectives	Core belief	Recruitment and selection	Retention	Succession planning	Development approach
Process	Include all processes to optimise people.	Competency based, consistent approach.	Good on processes, e.g. work–life balance.	Routine review process based on performance review cycle.	Personal development plans and reviews. Maybe some individual interventions.
Cultural	Belief that talent is needed for success.	Look for new talent. Allow introductions from in-house.	Allow people the freedom to demonstrate their talent, and to succeed and fail.	Develop in-house if possible. If not, look outside.	Individuals negotiate their own development paths. Coaching and mentoring are standard.
Competitive	Keep talent away from the competition.	Pay the best so you attract the best. Poach the best from the competition.	Good people like to work with good people. Aim to be employer of choice.	Geared towards retention – letting people know what their target jobs are.	Both planned and opportunistic approaches adopted. Mentors used to build loyalty.
Developmental	Accelerate development of high potentials.	Ideally only recruit at entry point and then develop.	Clear development paths and schemes to lock high potentials into career paths.	Identified groups will be developed for each level of the organisation.	Both planned and opportunistic.
HR planning	Right people in the right jobs at the right time.	Target areas of shortage across the company. Numbers and quotas approach.	Turnover expected, monitored and accounted for in plans.	Detailed in-house mappings for individuals.	Planned in cycles according to business needs.
Change management	Use talent management to instigate change in the organisation.	Seek out mavericks and change agents to join the organisation.	Projects and assignments keep change agents, but turnover of mainstay staff can occur.	Can be a bit opportunistic initially until change is embedded.	Change agents develop others who align with them and become the next generation of talent.

Table 2.4: Eighteen dimensions that affect the operational impact of talent management

Defining	Developing	Structures and systems
1. Size of talent pool	7. Development path	14. Performance management
2. Entry criteria	8. Development focus	
3. Decision process	9. Support	15. Talent management processes
4. Permanency of definition	10. Influence on career	
5. Recruitment as a source of talent	11. Connected conversations	16. Use of technology
	12. Organisational values	17. Systems flexibility
6. Transparency	13. Risk	18. Ownership of talent

The extent of ALD programmes

Brief accounts and examples of high-potential programmes in both the private and public sectors are given in Chapter 4, but how common are they? In the UK, for example, 50 per cent of organisations appear to have some form of talent management system; 35 per cent of managers think their organisation does not have such a system; and a further 15 per cent do not know (CMI and Ashridge Consulting, 2007). The situation is similar in Australia, for which we have more detailed information. Hudson (2007) surveyed over 7,000 employers about their high-potential and fast-track programmes and found that just over a half (52 per cent) reported that there was a formal scheme in place. Nearly one-third (31 per cent) reported no formal programme and about one-fifth (18 per cent) did not know. The survey of Australian schemes showed that there were some variations across sectors of business. For example, 60 per cent of employers in utilities, professional services and manufacturing reported the existence of formal programmes. Conversely, only 25 per cent of non-profit organisations and 38 per cent of government healthcare organisations indicated that they had formal programmes in place.

When asked about the management of high-potential programmes, 52 per cent of Australian employers indicated that they were run by HR departments; 25 per cent of programmes were run by individual business units; and a further 18 per cent by the executive team. Asked how they assessed someone's suitability for a high-potential programme, employers derived information from various sources: managers' ratings (37 per cent) or performance data (35 per cent) were more common than other assessment options such as 360-degree surveys (12 per cent), psychometric assessment (8 per cent) or assessment centres (5 per cent). The identification of 'talent' and selection for fast-track programmes is discussed further in the next chapter.

Hudson's research shows that organisations in Australia with high-potential programmes are using a number of strategies to develop people in the programme, including internal training and mentoring, external training, secondments, special projects and job rotations. This multifaceted approach indicates that a blend of development opportunities is much more effective than attempting to implement a one-size-fits-all (or one-size-fits-no-one) model.

The main benefits of their organisation's high-potential programme were also noted: 31 per cent of Australian employers said they used it for retaining and motivating key talent; just over a quarter (28 per cent) mentioned its ability to develop future leaders; and 24 per cent commented on its effect in succession planning/risk mitigation. Less than 1 per cent responded that their existing high-potential programme had little or no effect. Of the employers with no programme in place, or those who were unaware of one in their organisation, the majority (83 per cent) responded that this had a negative effect on the organisation.

Characteristics of high-potential and fast-track staff

In the last 20 years, research has begun to identify the key features of staff demonstrating high leadership potential. For example, Gritzmacher (1989) outlined nine key characteristics of fast-track/high-potential staff. These are:

1. A unique perception of their occupation: they see their daily activities fitting into a career pattern, rather than simply doing a job, and believe that their active leadership role is making the organisation stronger.
2. A broad thinking style: seeing wholes rather than job-bounded parts; seeing symbolic significances to actions.
3. Time consciousness: a drive to achieve the most as soon as possible; a drive to achieve a goal and embrace the next one.
4. Independence: a creative urge to add value to guidelines; a fast-learned knowledge of what would be good to accomplish.
5. High commitment: not wanting to miss out on anything interesting for the organisation; a belief that the organisation would be diminished without them and a drive to enact that self-perceived importance constructively.
6. High energy: the ability to get supra-normal amounts of work done and cheerfully come back for more.
7. A need for creativity and variety: they need new and testing challenges.
8. A varying interest in teamwork: the badging of fast trackers as the favoured sons and daughters can make team interplay difficult;

also the need to move ahead faster than the pack can make them impatient with others.

9. Continual improvement: a hunger to challenge and improve whatever they are involved in.

Other research, also carried out in the late 1980s, identified several psychological characteristics associated with fast trackers. Kovach (1989) concluded that those who showed high potential believed that:

- work is a primary source of satisfaction;
- time and energy can be stretched if managed well, i.e. as less finite resources than are usually portrayed;
- problems are really opportunities;
- self-responsibility is key.

Harris and Field (1992: 5) described fast trackers as follows:

> They itch to…get involved, make real contributions…they want visibility…these people want a challenge. High risk/high reward is what they are looking for.

In an earlier study, the same authors (Field and Harris, 1991) surveyed 276 identified fast trackers in an attempt to discover frustrations experienced on development programmes. They identified these as a lack of career planning and counselling, lack of perceived job challenge and responsibility, lack of developmental activities, and slow career progression.

Research by McCartney and Garrow (2006) shows that the highest performing employees (not necessarily fast-track staff) are far more productive than their lower-performing colleagues. Organisations operating such programmes see them as key to long-term organisational success. The highest-performing staff can be three times as productive (whether measured by quantitative or qualitative data on output) as poorly performing staff, which can make the investment in resources to identify and develop them a cost-effective one.

Research by Draycott (2003) carried out with high-potential staff in over 40 companies suggests that one of the key factors determining their commitment to the organisation is the quality of leadership they receive in the early years, e.g. quality of mentoring. This research also showed the following:

- High-potential staff differ from other staff in the way they view and interact with the organisation.
- Their commitment is determined by aspects of organisational functioning, rather than by their experience of the work environment, e.g. high-potential staff tend to be more concerned with opportunities for career development, the quality of career appraisals and their

experiences of leadership than other staff, for whom the focus is usually upon such factors as pay and working conditions.

- For high-potential staff, these organisational factors (including communication, customer focus, career development opportunities and employer image) consistently have a strong statistical relationship with measures of their commitment to the organisation.
- Their work experience had no statistical relationship to their organisational commitment. In leadership style, there were statistically significant differences in the value ascribed to certain leadership attributes, notably that high potential staff tend to value more highly a clear direction and clear values in the organisation, whereas other staff were more concerned with role models and respect for everyone's opinions.

Based upon their work with the RHR International 'Top Talent' programme, Kovach and Leonard (2003) suggested that, to give of their best, high-potential staff need feedback, a rigorous development plan, room to reflect upon and capture their learning, and a role that allows them to be fulfilled. Their research found no consistently common personality traits that determined the success of high-potential staff. They often all have the talent to progress, but it is the speed at which they progress that is determined by the development they receive. To accelerate the developmental process, the research suggests that high-potential staff need to have an appetite for learning, including the willingness to take risks, admit mistakes and weaknesses, and to learn from others.

In their work with high-flying staff in the private sector, Galpin and Skinner (2004) found that high-potential staff had significant differences in the factors that motivated them when compared to non-high-potential staff. For example, they:

- have a stronger work ethic;
- enjoy working hard;
- want to be dominant and to have influence;
- strive for excellence;
- have a concern with status;
- need challenge;
- need regular new tasks.

Although the research was conducted entirely within the private sector, the two areas where there were no significant differences between high-potential and other staff were the areas of 'acquisitiveness' and 'being competitive'. This supports other work in the area, suggesting that high-potential staff have stronger internal motivators and that financial rewards are not a key factor.

McCall (1998) suggests that high-potential staff have key learning factors that distinguish them. He found that they:

- learn quickly;
- integrate new information to direct future activity;
- adapt to new situations;
- have high levels of organisational commitment;
- develop high levels of job-specific knowledge;
- have an orientation towards learning from others;
- see new initiatives positively;
- take risks in their development and work;
- respond to feedback;
- learn from mistakes;
- are open to criticism.

Role of line managers

The effects of the personality of the staff member and their workplace are mitigated through the relationship with their line manager, or other managers having significant influence over their work. Kovach and Leonard (2003) found that the role of the line manager within the development of high-performing employees was critical; it was a key factor in accelerating and sustaining development. They found that the boss, together with the HR department, needed to be involved in the development processes. There was a need to match the high-potential member of staff to challenges. Their RHR International 'Top Talent' programme research suggests that competency frameworks are not the best way to achieve development. They support the idea that the contextual aspects of the role matter most. They state that it is more important for high-potential staff to be developed so that they are able to manage the kind of situations and environments that the future holds for them, rather than to develop competencies. Accordingly, the situations may be underpinned with behaviours, but not represented as 'competencies'. Kovach and Leonard support the work of others which found that the most compelling development takes place in work, rather than through courses or other formal training. The role of those people involved in the day-to-day management and support of high-potential staff, often their line managers, is therefore critical and deserves particular attention.

Although the RHR research could find no common factors within the traits of high-potential staff, Kovach and Leonard (2003) did find common 'derailment factors'. They noted that high-potential staff tended to be very action- and job-focused, and to move jobs within the organisation frequently, often not having to live with the consequences of their actions. This can be problematical, as they fail to address the 'people' issues behind the tasks and become what are called 'mile wide, inch deep managers'. Arrogant or insensitive dimensions of their behaviour become limiting as they move further up the organisation and this leads to their career being derailed. There are thought to be key inflection points in the careers of high-potential staff where these limitations are exposed, typically at the point where they move from functional roles into more strategic positions. There is a tendency to favour their old functional unit or discipline, and to have a restricted view of the wider business environment.

The National College, in one of its 'Evidence into Practice Guides' (*What are we learning about…identifying talent?* NCSL, 2009a), highlighted research carried out by the Hay Group which identifies potential 'derailing' forces capable of disrupting leadership development and causing potential to be overlooked. These forces, which manifest themselves at both the organisational and individual level, are set out in Table 2.5.

Table 2.5: Potential organisational and individual derailers

Potential organisational derailers		
Factor	Risk	Response
Career transition	Lack of support at key transitional stages (such as a first leadership role) when newly developed skills are tested in a real-life setting.	• Provide moral support • Peer-to-peer networking • Offer early feedback on impact • Create space for thinking and planning • Build confidence • Provide early support to newly appointed leaders
Changing job demands	Development is unresponsive to changing job demands and/or fails to equip individuals for new leadership roles of the future.	• Build in regular review of skills being developed • Focus development on transferable skills, e.g. ability to adapt and learn from others • Enable individuals to shape their own development to be context- specific

Potential individual derailers		
Factor	Risk	Response
Change in personal circumstances	Individual's priorities change in light of experience and/or unforeseen events.	Talent development programmes must allow for an appropriate level of wastage to take into account
Negative aspects of high potential traits	Individuals de-rail themselves through: • short-term achievement focus at expense of acquiring breadth of experience • arrogance • inability to listen • lack of self-awareness. There are sometimes negative dimensions of positive traits such as ambition, focus and self-confidence.	• Continued coach/ mentor support • Constructive feedback on performance

Summary

This chapter has examined the notion of accelerated leadership development and some of its attendant concepts such as talent management, leadership pipelines and acceleration pools. It has also shown how extensive ALD programmes are and has outlined the characteristics of high-potential and fast-track staff, highlighting the key role played by line managers. The next chapter continues the analysis and examines the approaches and methods associated with accelerated leadership development.

Chapter 3

Accelerated leadership development: Approaches and methods

- **Development opportunities**
- **Selecting individuals to fast track**
- **Methods for developing leaders**

Organisations employ a range of methods for developing those members of the workforce seen as having leadership talent or potential. While there is a huge range of development opportunities available, the most effective forms of leadership development are those centred on the actual job and hence the importance of the line manager as earlier noted. This chapter considers the main ways in which individuals are selected for accelerated or fast-track programmes as well as the various methods available for their development.

Development opportunities

A review of the literature suggests that the three most effective ways of developing people at work are coaching, work-based assignments and internal training. A number of organisations favoured a tailored approach towards meeting individuals' needs and levels of experience. Some also preferred a self-managed approach to development, placing emphasis on individuals to show greater initiative in relation to their career enhancement. Approaches to developing people on accelerated leadership development (ALD) and fast track programmes are likely to include some of the following:

- assessment/development/acceleration centres;
- psychometric testing and 360-degree appraisal;
- challenging, real projects and work-based assignments;
- coaching with real experiences;
- role models and mentoring;

- role rotation;
- regular and constructive feedback;
- leadership and management courses;
- reflective writing and journals;
- action learning sets;
- blended/e-learning (personalisation).

Selecting individuals to fast track

A key decision for organisations is whether to provide employees with accelerated development opportunities, to fast track them into senior roles, or to provide gradual development, thus allowing employees time to gain experience of different roles. The previous chapter noted how suitability for high-potential programmes was often derived from line managers' ratings, performance data, 360-degree feedback surveys, psychometric assessment and assessment centres. Different organisations select individuals using some or all of the above criteria and to differing extents. Table 3.1 illustrates the ways in which three well-known companies select specific groups of employees for fast tracking when there is a business need.

Table 3.1: Selection of fast-track participants – three examples

Organisation	Selection strategy
Fujitsu	To illustrate Fujitsu's approach, they set up a fast-track development scheme to fill the business-critical role of Account Manager, responsible for securing business on high-value accounts. They created an intensive 12-month development programme to support and develop individuals so that they could take up their position within 3–12 months.
Royal & Sun Alliance	The company runs an International Fast Track programme that recruits young, dynamic and talented second jobbers, usually of MBA calibre, into specific roles across the organisation. It also offers a fast-track package of development and exposure with a six-month international assignment. Fast Track is open to internal candidates who show potential to be international leaders of the future.

Lloyds TSB	Lloyds TSB adopt a leadership pipeline, which emphasises building experience as opposed to fast tracking. This means that individuals are able to move from one part of the pipeline to another, i.e. move from 'managing others' to 'managing managers'. The company uses a Career Paths Tool that helps to assess (through self- and management-assessment) whether an individual is ready to make the next turn at a leadership level and what development experience is required to get them there.

In its publication, *What are we learning about…identifying talent?*, the National College (NCSL, 2009a: 5) suggests asking the following questions for planning local talent development programmes:

- Is the programme focused on those leadership behaviours that are likely to have the greatest impact on student learning?
- Is there absolute clarity of expectations for everyone involved in the programme?
- Is there an explicit performance management process for those individuals taking part in the programme?
- Is the proposed programme sensitive to the needs of potential leaders of different phases?
- Where coaches or mentors are being used, is there a clear quality assurance and performance management mechanism in place?
- How does the programme allow for personalisation?
- How does the programme support diversity among future school leaders?
- How does the programme help build the future pipeline of leadership talent?

Fink (2010), based on his research and extensive educational experience, 'offer[s] the following questions about potential leadership candidates as [a]… guide to determining who should be recruited for leadership roles':

- Does this person genuinely like and respect the students?
- Is this person a dedicated and proficient teacher?
- Is this person committed to learning for *all* students?
- Does this person operate from a life affirming set of values and have the courage of his or her convictions?
- Has this person initiated professional growth activities to enhance his or her personal abilities – reason, ethics, imagination, intuition, memory and common sense?
- Has this person the intellectual and relational potential to master the meta-learnings for leadership such as 'understanding learning',

'critical thinking', 'futures thinking', 'contextual knowledge', 'political acumen', 'emotional understanding' and 'making connections'?
- Does this person have the organizational skills to manage a school or department?
- Does this person relate well to colleagues? To parents? To superiors in the organization?
- Does this person have a tolerance for ambiguity?
- Does this person have a strong work ethic and a well-developed 'crap detector'?

(Fink, 2010: 171)

Methods for developing leaders

As earlier noted, organisations make use of an assortment of methods for developing their workforce on accelerated leadership development and talent management programmes: for example, providing feedback, coaching, mentoring, redesigning jobs, setting stretch assignments, and conventional training. According to McCall (1998), ALD experiences can be sorted into four broad categories, from which he was able to identify 16 different developmental experiences, as shown in Table 3.2.

Table 3.2: Developmental experiences

Category	Developmental experiences
On-the-job	• Assignments • Early work experiences • First-time supervision • Building something from nothing • Fix it/turn it around • Project/task force • Increase in job scope
Hardship and setbacks (learning from experience)	• Ideas: failure and mistakes • Demotions/missed promotions • Subordinate performance problem • Breaking a rut • Personal traumas

Working with other people (specifically hierarchical superiors)	• Role models (superiors with exceptional qualities) • Values playing out (snapshots of senior leadership behaviour that demonstrates corporate values)
Other events	• Coursework (formal courses) • Purely personal (experiences outside work)

In their survey of more than 50 companies in the UK, Oliver and Vincent (2000) found the three most effective ways of developing people at work were coaching, work-based assignments and internal training. The Centre for Organisational Research (2001) recognised several characteristics of high-impact leadership development schemes. These schemes:

- use action and experiential learning to develop an authentic learning process;
- encourage leaders to assume responsibility for planning and implementing their own learning experiences to meet their needs;
- encourage development at three levels: self, team and organisation;
- have a core mission statement or all-encompassing purpose around which the system and programmes are built, which drives all initiatives and behaviours, is aligned with corporate strategy and is clearly communicated to all staff;
- provide development experiences that involve innovation, creativity, strategising and thinking 'outside the box';
- build a culture that is supportive of leadership development at all levels;
- encourage multi-disciplinary experiences to drive 'breakthrough thinking' and innovation (through job rotations, global assignments, development assignments);
- use formal and/or internal mentoring to help develop leaders;
- assess the development of leaders from all perspectives (peer reviews, review by superior and subordinates);
- use technology and e-learning.

Although many organisations invest heavily in talent management programmes, there is a range of low-cost – even no-cost – opportunities that can be utilised, particularly when resources are scarce. For example, activities such as networking opportunities, mentoring and coaching from senior management, and job shadowing, have proved to cost relatively little. A low-cost strategy successfully adopted by organisations involves encouraging talent to share learning and to develop together. Action learning sets are used by several companies who also ensure that employees returning from external events feed back and share their learning with others. Senior executives run action learning sets with small groups of employees, covering topics such as effectively leading teams and handling crises.

A number of organisations have created their own Assessment and Development Centres:

- One company, a bank, runs an intensive 3½-day Development Centre for their business leadership programme and makes use of some of its managing directors as observer coaches to provide immediate feedback and some role-modelling for aspirants to the role.
- An engineering firm has a Centre devoted to Director Development for top-level managers who are likely to make Director in the next 2–3 years and a Management Development Centre for people expected to progress to senior management.
- An insurance company offers involvement in business-driven 'real' projects, many of which result in new processes, procedures and products.

Research carried out by Roffey Park (2004) found that their four case-study organisations used a range of methods to develop leaders. These included:

- training and development programmes;
- formal qualifications;
- experiential learning;
- long-term global assignments;
- international teams and forums;
- mentoring and coaching;
- increasing self-awareness;
- tailoring development.

Like other research, Galpin and Skinner's (2004) study found the most effective forms of development were those centred on the actual job. High-flyers and fast-trackers valued the chance to change roles frequently; feedback on their progress; and the ongoing help provided by their mentor.

In a study of European companies, Mabey and Ramirez (2004) ranked HR department and line-manager preferences for accelerated leadership development methods as follows:

- internal skills programmes;
- external courses, seminars and conferences;
- mentoring/coaching;

- formal qualifications;
- in-company job rotation;
- external assignments, placements and/or secondments;
- e-learning.

In all the European companies studied, there was a relatively low preference for on-the-job development, e.g. job rotation and assignments, and a strikingly low uptake of e-learning. Within the UK, there was a higher than average use of qualifications-based development.

Bolden (2005) proposed the following most prevalent forms of leadership development:

- leadership courses;
- facilitated workshops;
- coaching, counselling and mentoring;
- reflective writing and journals;
- action learning;
- role play and simulations;
- leadership exchange;
- psychometric testing;
- 360-degree appraisal;
- leadership consultancy;
- e-learning.

Hudson's (2007) ongoing research with Australian organisations has shown that there are key elements to a successful high-potential leadership development programme. In summary, organisations should define their strategy and future business needs and then develop clear talent identification criteria, incorporate an assessment process and equip their high-potential staff for future leadership roles. There is also a need to establish a high-potential committee and communicate with and obtain buy-in from executives and managers. Hudson also states that organisations should be ready for their high performers to wax and wane in performance; and to review the fast-track programme regularly and make it accountable, with key performance indicators or success criteria.

As will be shown in Part 2, many of the above forms of leadership development are currently found in the education sector, although the extent to which the different forms are practised is unknown. The next chapter offers some further examples of fast-track programmes from both the private and public sectors.

Chapter 4

High-potential programmes: Examples from the private and public sectors

- **Lessons from other sectors**
- **Leadership development approaches**
- **High-potential programmes**

This chapter briefly outlines the main lessons that can be learned from the experiences of sectors outside education, while also considering approaches to developing leaders and the content of high-potential programmes. Concise examples from five private and public sector organisations from outside England are also given.

Lessons from other sectors

A study of a range of organisations in different sectors (e.g. Lloyds TSB, Grant Thornton, Waitrose, Accenture, Network Rail) was conducted by the Chartered Management Institute and Ashridge Consulting (2007). A number of the conclusions concerned the design and delivery of high-potential programmes and the support structures and systems needed. These are shown in Table 4.1.

Table 4.1: Characteristics of talent management schemes in all sectors

Defining talent	• Talent management is about doing something additional or different with those people who are defined as talent for the purpose of the organisation. • In the UK, 50 per cent of organisations appear to have some form of talent management system.

	• The vast majority of UK managers (84 per cent) want to be considered high potential, and for these managers qualifications were the most significant factor to them in terms of how they were managing their careers.
	• Those who think their organisation considers them to be talented/high potential are significantly more motivated by their career and the direction of the organisation.
	• Being identified as talent in UK organisations means more pressure, enhanced development opportunities and better promotion. Very few managers (7 per cent) believed it resulted in resentment among peers.
	• Over 60 per cent of UK managers agreed that those identified as high potential or talented were expected to become senior managers/partners, suggesting that a permanent definition prevails in UK organisations.
	• There are advantages and disadvantages arising from having a transparent talent system. Clearly it is important not to raise expectations if an organisation is unable to deliver for individuals.
Developing talent	• Promotions, project work, management training schemes and management qualifications were the main development opportunities offered and undertaken in organisations.
	• Secondments, transfers and shadowing opportunities were offered by many organisations, but few managers had personal experience of these development routes. Because of the absence of any significant differences found between those opportunities undertaken between managers who would like to be considered 'talent-rated' and those who would not, it suggests that many organisations are not differentiating development routes in reality.
	• For managers who wished to be considered as talent-rated, qualifications, having the right coach/mentor, appropriate training courses, internal networking and taking on larger teams, were regarded as important for their future career development.
	• Unlike their international counterparts, many UK managers appeared reluctant to change roles or move abroad.

	• The relationship between line managers and those identified as talent requires sensitive management in terms of who should take responsibility for the individual's development.
	• Where the development of high-potential staff takes place in a highly supportive culture, the risks associated with allocating stretching assignments or role transfers can be significantly mitigated.
Support structures and systems	• Performance management systems provide a good baseline for talent management systems on the basis of performance, although many systems are not geared towards measuring an individual's potential and future capability. Only about one-third of managers (31 per cent) were confident that their appraisal system was capable of identifying high-potential staff.
	• The talent decision-making process rests between senior managers and line managers, with just under 30 per cent of organisations allowing individuals to contribute to the decision themselves.
	• Most organisations see the need for a more central ownership approach to talent in order to get senior management buy-in and strategic alignment with the programme.
	• Most organisations are concerned with some measure of return on investment with regard to talent management, but not many are maintaining records or IT systems that would give them data to measure any returns.

Leadership development approaches

A number of organisations favoured a tailored or customised approach towards meeting individuals' needs and levels of experience. They recognised that a 'one-size-fits-all' approach was not appropriate. Some also preferred a self-managed approach to development, placing emphasis on individuals to show greater initiative in relation to their career enhancement. Table 4.2 illustrates the leadership development approach used by four private sector organisations in the UK in the mid-2000s.

Table 4.2: Leadership development methods

Organisation	Leadership development approach
Abbey	Because of the many variables around people's functional and management ability, their experience, style and preference, Abbey believes in a 'horses for courses' approach, thus rejecting the strategy of exposing everyone to an identical experience.
Royal & Sun Alliance	Specific talent streams are set up which offer varied, individually focused development opportunities matched to the organisation's strategic imperatives.
Lilly UK	Every employee is equipped with a personal development plan covering a future span of 2–3 years. The organisation offers an extensive catalogue of programmes and online resources (toolkit and website). It also encourages employees to seek out their own opportunities within the organisation.
Lloyds TSB	The needs of the individual drive the development agenda. The company uses a modular structure on issues common to all, which is then supplemented by a bespoke element.

Source: McCartney and Garrow, 2006.

High-potential programmes

We now offer some concise examples of organisations, in both the private and public sectors outside England, which are managing the succession management and talent process and offering high-potential, fast-track or accelerated leadership development programmes.

Example 1: Minnesota Department of Transportation (Min-DOT)

In operation since 1990, the succession management process in Min-DOT is reported as having achieved some success, largely because of the acceptance and support it has received across the agency. An agency-wide working group identified strategic positions of significance to the health of the organisation. Based on a voluntary survey, potential successors are identified and an assessment of individuals and organisational needs occurs. This includes a review of the high-potential individuals' personal and work histories, structured meetings that review management talent from unit through to department level and competency profiling (through manager and self-perceptions) of the potential successors. Based on this information, individuals under consideration are rated on potential and readiness for strategic positions in which they have expressed interest. A group of individuals is chosen for individual development through a variety of methodologies (including job reassignments). Those who are not chosen are given feedback on where they need to develop for future consideration.

Example 2: American Greetings Corporation (AGC)

AGC set up a high-level management team to identify high-potential candidates for the top three management levels of the company (125 positions). Recommendations are made to this team by senior managers, who are required to provide evidence to support their nominations. A range of assessment techniques determines the competencies of the high-potential employees. Any competency gaps become the focus of development tasks created by the management team. Once the development tasks/projects are completed, the employee gives a presentation on the results of the project. AGC believes in the 'talent pool' approach because the company cannot be sure what positions will exist in the future. It also develops a sense of opportunity in a broad range of employees, which provides an incentive to 'stick around'. At AGC, the human resources department is intimately involved in the succession management process, cementing its role as a strategic partner with management by ensuring a steady stream of quality leadership in the organisation.

Example 3: The New Zealand State Services Commission

The New Zealand State Services Commission published guidelines for succession in the public service in October 1998. The fundamentals of its approach are:

1. Commitment from the chief executive officer;
2. A strategy in place which:
   (a) reflects early identification of potential,
   (b) is based on individual development plans,
   (c) is tied to the organisation's Key Results Areas and Strategic Results Areas;
3. Individual development plans focusing on competency gaps identified through a 'careful' assessment of competencies;
4. Creation of a variety of development opportunities;
5. An evaluation of the effectiveness of development activities.

Example 4: Western Australian Department of Resources Development (DRD)

This state government department is moving towards introducing a more systematic approach to the management of succession within the organisation. It is critical for a knowledge-based organisation like the DRD to have a pool of competent and experienced employees to handle its various and complex projects. Examination of the Department's age demographics prompted a review of the need for a managed succession plan. It was recognised that the Department needed to maintain a core of permanent, knowledgeable and experienced staff. Current recruitment tactics alongside the use of contract staff and consultants have partly achieved this, but it is acknowledged that they may not be sufficient. As a direct response, DRD has instituted a number of initiatives aimed at supporting and encouraging the development of staff in line with organisational objectives. To date, these include graduate recruitment, industry secondments, overseas exchange programmes and a comprehensive Performance Development Programme. The Department's Human Resources Strategic Plan has been developed as a key component of the Department's overall strategic planning approach and shows a clear commitment to 'support and encourage its staff'. Issues being confronted include the management of aspiring employees by providing opportunities for them to remain motivated to face future challenges. To address these types of issues, various initiatives were considered, including team-based work and changes to organisational structure. In looking towards the future, succession planning linked to high-potential development programmes was seen as only one way to ensure that an organisation has the right people. Other strategies needed to be considered, including knowledge transfer and a work environment conducive to learning.

Example 5: Police Service in Scotland

In common with other commercial and public sector organisations, the Scottish Police Service is concerned to ensure that those who will lead the Service in the future are suitably identified and prepared for their role. Whereas the opportunity to progress exists for all officers who demonstrate potential, a 'fast track' has been formed for those individuals who show particular talent and promise. This fast-track route, known as the Accelerated Promotion Scheme for Graduates (APSG), provides a structured career path for the most promising and capable graduates entering the police force.

The vast majority of graduates entering the Scottish Police Service do so as standard (non-APSG) entrants. For these graduates there is an opportunity to apply for the APSG during the initial two-year probationary period if they wish to do so. Additionally, officers are recruited onto the scheme from within the Service at both Constable and Sergeant level and mainstream opportunities to advance exist for those who demonstrate ability.

After gaining grounding in police work, the graduates' potential is developed with an emphasis on substantial responsibility early in their career. A programme, comprising six phases, provides a structure that allows career development from the rank of Constable to Chief Inspector and identifies officers ready for promotion to Superintendent. It is possible to attain the rank of Superintendent within about nine years' service. It is anticipated that a number of those individuals who complete the APSG programme will go on to hold Chief Officer rank.

It is stressed that the APSG offers an accelerated route to senior management – not a bypass. An individual who wishes to gain success and advancement within the police management must first make the grade as an effective and capable uniformed operational Constable involved in all the activities contained within that role.

The attributes listed below are among those considered prerequisites for effective leaders within the police:

- the ability to demonstrate clarity and speed of thought and action in routine and crisis situations, and sound judgement based on coherent thought processes;
- innovation and initiative: the creation of solutions to problems.
- learning skills that allow the rapid assimilation of the knowledge and experience that contribute to the make-up of an effective police officer;
- a commitment to the ethos and organisational values of the Scottish police service;
- the ability to communicate effectively, both verbally and in writing, externally to all members of society and internally at all levels of the organisation;
- a willingness to fully contribute to team performance whether as a follower or as a leader.

If selected for the police, whether as an APSG or standard entrant, recruits are allocated to a particular area and after training they will work a shift system, be part of a team and patrol either on foot or by car. They will be initially accompanied by a Tutor Constable, who will assist and advise them. Entrants making an application for the APSG are subject to the entry requirements and selection process for the force of their choice. The selection process includes the standard entrance test, background enquiries, interviews and fitness test medical checks.

Summary

Accelerated leadership development programmes are not uncommon in organisations in both private and public sectors in the UK and elsewhere, and this chapter has offered some brief examples of how such schemes operate. However, while it is helpful and interesting to know how matters are dealt with in other sectors and other countries there is a limit to what can be replicated or transferred successfully to the education system in England or elsewhere. The English education system is a highly decentralised one in which schools have a considerable degree of autonomy. As we show in Part 2, some interesting fast-track developments have taken place within individual schools and local authorities as well as those centrally delivered.

PART 2

ACCELERATED LEADERSHIP DEVELOPMENT IN SCHOOLS

Chapter 5

Accelerating the development of school staff

- **Development methods and approaches in schools**
- **Content of leadership development programmes**
- **How do leaders learn and develop?**
- **Development methods and approaches in schools**

That school leaders are critically important in bringing about successful schools is in little doubt (Day *et al.*, 2009; Pont *et al.*, 2008; Robinson *et al.*, 2008). Yet, little is known about the features of leadership programmes that lead to sustained school improvement and enhanced pupil outcomes. Interest in leadership development in both the private and public sectors is certainly not new but, as we discussed in Chapter 1, there seems to be little doubt that the profile of leadership development has risen dramatically recently both in the UK and internationally.

Development methods and approaches in schools

In England, the surge of interest in leadership development has been reflected in the expansion of programmes designed by universities, local authorities, schools and others, for example the National College for Leadership of Schools and Children's Services. Since its inception, the National College (formerly NCSL) has become 'a very significant part of the educational landscape and a major influence, arguably the major influence, on school leadership, management and administration in England and beyond' (Bush, 2004: 243). However, as well as providing or commissioning external leadership development programmes, the College has also given great emphasis to the role of the school in developing leaders. Schools are seen as needing to take a more proactive stance to talent development, and the College contends that 'we need to become much better at identifying potential leaders and finding ways to accelerate their development at the school and local system levels' (NCSL, 2007a: 9).

In schools, the development of leadership ability has been linked with strategies such as coaching, networking, and the distribution of leadership responsibilities. Given the imperative to grow future leaders rapidly, pressure has been placed upon schools to become more proactive and to put themselves forward as training grounds for leadership development. Developing leadership talent is an essential part of capacity building to ensure that schools have sufficient numbers of high-calibre leaders and that leadership development is a priority from an early stage in a teacher's career.

Some schools have given great attention to their staff development processes and procedures and have developed ways to grow their own leaders from within. In this chapter we draw upon relevant literature from both the private and public sectors, as well as from a growing body of relevant research and writing from the National College, to examine some of the various forms this has taken within schools. We consider both workplace – or on-the-job opportunities – and other forms of leadership development beyond the place of employment – workshops and off-the-job opportunities. Leadership development is often considered to be part of an off-site programme or course away from the workplace. It is to such external programmes that we first turn before considering more work-based forms of leader and leadership development in schools. The best programmes try to benefit from the strengths of both workplace and workshop learning.

Content of leadership development programmes

School leadership and management programmes, many of which are off-site, invariably cover a number of common elements and these are likely to include notions of leadership (including vision, mission and transformational leadership); learning and teaching (or learning-centred leadership); human resource management and development; financial management; and the management of external relations. But, despite the abundance of off-site leadership development programmes, there remains a significant question about their degree of congruence with the contemporary needs of schools. In a commercial context, Taylor *et al.* (2002: 149) argued that, 'the global changes now occurring demand approaches to leadership education that are profoundly different from those that have served well in the past'. Their contention is that these changes necessitate a reversal of six traditional priorities:

- from theory to practice;
- from part to systems;
- from states and roles to processes;

- from knowledge to learning;
- from individual knowledge to partnerships;
- from detached analysis to reflexive understanding.

Table 5.1 illustrates how this impacts upon leadership development programme structure and content.

Table 5.1: Key trends in leadership development programmes

Key trends	From	To
The programme	• Prescribed course • Standard • Theoretical	• Study programme and real issues • Customised • Theory in context
The time-frame	• One-off event	• A journey with ongoing support
The mode	• Lecturing/ listening • Conceptual	• Participatory, interactive and applied • Experiential and conceptual
The focus	• Individuals	• Individuals within a group, for a purpose
The consultant	• Supplier	• Partner, co-designer, facilitator, coach

Source: Bolden (2007). The Innovation Unit (www.innovationunit.org) has now developed this model further.

In education, a review in the USA of the leadership preparation literature (Darling-Hammond *et al.,* 2007) points to a number of important features of leadership development programmes, including:

- research-based content that is aligned with professional standards and focused on instruction, organisational development and change management;
- curricular coherence that links goals, learning activities and assessments around a set of shared values, beliefs and knowledge about effective organisational practice;
- field-based internships that enable candidates to apply leadership knowledge and skills under the guidance of an expert practitioner;
- problem-based learning strategies, such as case methods, action research and projects, that link theory and practice and support reflection;
- cohort structures that enable collaboration, teamwork and mutual support;

- mentoring or coaching that supports modelling, questioning, observations of practice and feedback;
- collaboration between universities and school districts to create coherence between training and practice as well as pipelines for recruitment, preparation, hiring and induction.

The research team found the best programmes made good use of the workplace as a site for leadership learning (Darling-Hammond *et al.,* 2009). How, then, do leaders learn best and develop their skills as leaders?

How do leaders learn and develop?

In 2001, the National College for School Leadership set out a national framework for leadership development that provides a professional development route for the preparation, induction, development and regeneration of school leaders. The framework identifies five stages of school leadership:

1. Emergent leadership – when a teacher takes on management and leadership responsibilities for the first time;
2. Established leadership – experienced leaders, e.g. assistant and deputy heads, who do not intend to pursue headship;
3. Entry to leadership – a teacher's preparation for and induction into a senior leadership post in the school;
4. Advanced leadership – mature school leaders (after 3–4 years in the role);
5. Consultant leadership – able and experienced leaders taking on the training, mentoring and coaching of other headteachers (NCSL, 2001).

Despite not being a linear system, these five stages have encouraged members of the profession to think in terms of progression routes for teachers aspiring to headship. The establishment of a national framework has encouraged exploration of new and innovative ideas around leadership development, for example distributed leadership, leaders as lead learners, and collaborative leadership. These five stages, and the leadership development opportunities available within each, are outlined elsewhere (Bubb and Earley, 2007).

It makes little sense to discuss ways of developing leaders or stages of school leadership development without also considering the manner in which leaders learn. Speck and Knipe (2005) provide an overview of what is known about the characteristics of professional development that lead to high levels of adult learning. They found that adult learners:

- will commit to learning when they believe that the objectives are realistic and important for their personal and professional needs;

- want to be responsible for their own learning and should therefore have some control over the what, who, how, why, when and where of their learning;
- need direct, concrete experiences for applying what they have learned to their work;
- do not automatically transfer learning into daily practice and often benefit from coaching and other kinds of follow-up support to sustain learning;
- need feedback on the results of their efforts;
- come to the learning process with self-direction and a wide range of previous experiences, knowledge, interests and competencies.

The Centre for Organisational Research (2001) identified a number of principles embodying high-impact leadership development systems or approaches that help leadership learning. It found that effective leadership development programmes made use of action and experiential learning to make the learning process 'real'; they encouraged leaders to take responsibility for planning and implementing their own learning experiences to meet their needs; development was encouraged at three levels: self, team and organisation; they had a core mission statement or all-encompassing purpose around which the system and programmes were built, which drives all initiatives and behaviours, is aligned with corporate strategy and is clearly communicated to all staff.

The Centre also found that successful leadership development programmes provided a culture that was supportive of leadership development at all levels and they encouraged multi-disciplinary experiences 'to drive breakthrough thinking and innovation' (through such activities as job rotations, global assignments and development assignments). They also made use of mentoring to help leaders develop leaders and they assessed the development of leaders from a number of different perspectives (e.g. peer reviews, review by superior and subordinates). Finally, they found that high-impact leadership development systems or approaches made good use of technology and e-learning.

McCall (1998) identified 16 different developmental experiences that were found to have significant impact on leader development. These are shown in Table 5.2 grouped under four headings: early experiences/assorted; hardship and setbacks; other people; and other events. McCall's list comprises a wide variety of activities, other than formal training programmes, capable of impacting on the development of leaders. His work also highlights the importance of presenting these leadership development opportunities at an early stage in people's careers.

Table 5.2: Developmental experiences with impact

Early experiences/assorted
- Assignments
- Early work experiences
- First-time supervision
- Building something from nothing
- Fix it/turn it around
- Project/task force
- Increase in job scope

Hardship and setbacks
- Ideas: failure and mistakes
- Demotions/missed promotions
- Subordinate performance problem
- Breaking a rut
- Personal traumas

Other people
- Role models (superiors with exceptional qualities)
- Values playing out (snapshots of senior leadership behaviour that demonstrates corporate values)

Other events
- Coursework (formal course)
- Purely personal (experiences outside work)

Source: McCall (1998). Reprinted with permission from *People & Strategy (Journal of HRPS)*, 1998 12-1. Copyright 2010. All rights reserved.

Drawing on research involving managers in sectors outside education, Thomson *et al.* (2001) refer to a range of leadership development methods that are perceived to be effective. These methods include:

- on-the-job training and in-house training;
- coaching and mentoring;
- the use of consultants;
- formal induction;
- job rotation.

Similarly, a study by Sandler (2002) of around 400 organisations worldwide found that leadership capability was enhanced using external and internal leadership programmes, such as: temporary 'stretch' assignments; international assignments; external consultants; job rotation; demanding assignments to develop management skills; and formal mentoring. There would appear to be clear implications from these research findings for school leadership development, not least the low ranking of formal training.

High levels of adult learning about school leadership can occur as a result of attending an off-site training programme or because of the learning opportunities created within the workplace, using a range of the above methods. Indeed, the best leadership development is that which makes use of several methods in a complementary and reciprocal manner. For example, when heads were asked what they perceived to be the *single* most powerful development opportunity of their career in helping to forge their understanding of school leadership, both 'on-the-job' development opportunities such as working with others, especially a good role model, and 'off-the-job' development opportunities, such as postgraduate study, were noted as highly significant (Earley and Weindling, 2004). But is enough being done within the workplace to ensure the development of the next generation of school leaders? Are schools increasingly taking on this leadership development role and what should they be doing to ensure that the supply of leaders does not dry up?

Development methods and approaches in schools

In contrast to commercial organisations, little is known about accelerated leadership development methods and experiences in schools. We have a growing body of literature about effective leadership development (see NCSL, 2008a) but less so concerning the fast tracking of potential school leaders. Traditionally, local authority personnel, for example advisers and inspectors, have been influential in identifying talented teachers and assisting with, or sponsoring, their career development and promotion. Talent-spotting and sponsorship were seen as part of the (then) Local Education Authority adviser's role, although perhaps not always written explicitly into job descriptions. Today, partly in response to the National College's succession planning strategy with its emphasis on local solutions, a growing number of local authorities are developing 'Future Leaders' or 'Leaders of Tomorrow' programmes, some elements of which involve talent-spotting and an emphasis on accelerated development. In addition, some secondary schools have worked as federations or have collaborated in order to provide accelerated programmes for their high-potential staff.

In the UK, some studies have provided insights into leadership succession issues. For example, Fletcher-Campbell (2003) gathered teacher perspectives on the advantages, or otherwise, of aspiring to middle-leader roles, and Earley *et al.* (2002) sought views on the appeal of headship. Castagnoli and Cook (2004) emphasised the importance of training new staff in order to replace other staff as they leave. Hayes (2005) cautioned that the number of deputy heads seeking headship was falling. In Scotland, Draper and McMichael (2003) and more recently MacBeath *et al.* (2009) also found reluctance among senior staff to take on the added responsibilities associated with headship.

A report produced by the National College (NCSL, 2007c) draws on the outcomes of a study investigating how school leaders actively encourage and secure future leadership capacity by identifying, nurturing and developing leadership potential in their schools. Over the years some schools have been seen as 'training grounds for heads', where heads took great pride in the number of deputies they were able to 'train up' for headship (Weindling and Earley, 1987). However, what seems to be needed now is for all schools to adopt such an approach and become learning-centred and to be concerned for the development and training of all their staff. The importance of providing learning opportunities for all staff who work in schools – the school workforce – has been reflected in government policy and through the work of the Training and Development Agency for Schools (TDA) (see Bubb and Earley, 2010). Schools with a strong staff development culture are sometimes called professional learning communities (Bolam *et al.*, 2005) or learning-centred (Bubb and Earley, 2007); the National College refers to schools that have adopted this proactive stance as 'Greenhouse Schools' (2006). Through a case-study approach, the National College report builds on previous literature that had earlier identified the issues around succession planning (e.g. Hartle and Thomas, 2003; Creasy *et al.*, 2004; Hartle, 2005). The proposed strategies for growing tomorrow's leaders are to:

- start identifying potential leaders at the recruitment and selection stage;
- see in-post identification as a mixture of formal and informal processes and raise awareness that everyone is a leader;
- know what you are looking for in developing leadership potential;
- offer opportunities for aspiring and developing leaders to take a lead and/or set up within the school and learn from this through reflection;
- provide systems such as buddying, mentoring, coaching, shadowing or team-based working to support professional growth;
- provide local solutions in collaboration with others, e.g. schools or external bodies;
- promote an ethos that makes a clear statement about investing in the individual;
- develop support structures such as training plan discussions that enable individual and team growth;
- look beyond the school for local, national and international opportunities for leadership development;

- plan strategically, both within and across individual schools, to allow for the development of internal capacity and succession, while at the same time taking into account individuals' career needs and those of the system.

(Adapted from NCSL, 2006: 16–17)

In *Greenhouse Schools* (NCSL, 2006), examples are given of how school leaders actively encourage and secure future leadership capacity by identifying, nurturing and developing leadership potential in their schools. The case studies show that worthwhile approaches have emerged. For example, when asked to highlight ways in which their schools identify leadership potential, action was taken at two levels – prior to appointment and following appointment (see Table 5.3).

Table 5.3: Greenhouse Schools – developing potential

What schools did prior to appointment	What schools did post-appointment
• Assess the potential of final practice students at the school in relation to future opportunities for employment. • Adopt a policy of wording advertisements so that potential applicants were aware that they were being invited to 'teach and learn at…'. • Focus the recruitment process upon specific criteria, one of which was 'an ability to learn and share'. • Trawl applications for evidence of prior leadership experience when short-listing in order to identify people who have actually shown some interest in leadership.	• Conduct pre-determined, day-to-day informal observations of colleagues at work: assess how they work with others and respond to different situations. • Attach senior leaders to departments as internal consultants to aid their professional knowledge of leadership potential. • Provide opportunities for teachers to try out leadership in the context of, for example, a specific project or task. • Carry out less formal career chats in addition to performance management. • Monitor classroom practice. • Observe contributions at meetings. • Track staff participation in leading extra-curricular and voluntary activities.

Source: adapted from NCSL, 2006: 8–9.

Having identified leadership potential, the case study schools nurtured and developed them by:

- providing leaders with space to try things out and learn from their efforts;
- offering support but encouraging independence;
- enabling leaders to operate within a no-blame, yet accountable, culture of trust and autonomy;
- offering external professional development opportunities, e.g. Master's programmes, outreach work, international visits, NCSL programmes;
- providing internal training and development such as:
  - school-based middle management programmes;
  - training plans for teachers produced in consultation with line managers;
  - 'outstanding teacher' programmes – one school offered a twilight immersion programme run by staff and offering outreach work both locally and abroad;
  - in-house leadership courses aimed at those aspiring to either middle or senior leadership;
  - external consultants supporting in-house leadership programmes and self-evaluation;
  - induction programmes for new teachers providing basic training and the allocation of a mentor;
  - formalised opportunities for discussions focused on leadership – one school supported these with academic articles or think pieces;
  - opportunities to carry out research projects;
- providing internal role development opportunities such as:
  - funded temporary acting-up opportunities;
  - other acting-up opportunities, e.g. in response to headteacher secondment;
  - shared leadership opportunities, e.g. the appointment of joint post-holders;
  - bespoke posts to match specific areas of leadership potential;
  - opportunities to participate in working parties;
- offering coaching and mentoring such as:
  - shadowing post-holders;
  - constructive feedback on leadership actions;
  - pastoral mentorship for new staff members into school or post;
  - professional mentorship, usually the line manager, for all staff;
  - peer coaching;
  - buddy systems to allow teachers to develop leadership skills by working with other colleagues.

(NCSL, 2006: 10–11)

The same study (NCSL, 2006: 15–16) suggests that the strategies the schools had put into practice to develop leadership potential could be transferred. However, the extent of their effectiveness would be dependent upon a school having in place such things as an understanding of its own context and state of readiness; a headteacher with a vision for leadership development; a critical mass of those committed to the development of such practices; leaders with the capacity to develop and implement appropriate strategies; an innovative ethos; trusting relationships; a collective sense of responsibility; and a willingness to share and learn and consider how external practices can transfer to a new context.

Summary

The Hay Group (2007, cited in Barnes, 2008) have identified four opportunities that help accelerate leaders' growth. They provide a useful summary of this chapter. They are:

1. job shadowing to observe and work closely with more senior leaders;
2. job rotation, where people work in unfamiliar functions or contexts;
3. participation and consultation on organisation-wide initiatives;
4. mentoring and coaching to support the interpretation of experience.

Also, it is important to note that accelerating development means 'not only giving them opportunities within school but also, for example, offering them the chance to work in a range of different contexts – urban, rural, multi-ethnic, large, small – so that they emerge as leaders with a breadth of expertise and experience' (NCSL, 2008a: 9).

Clearly, there is much taking place regarding leadership development and succession planning. However, it is not clear from the case-study examples in *Greenhouse Schools* the degree to which the identified talented individuals are fast tracked. The cases offered are examples of effective leadership development programmes which may or may not involve a degree of accelerated progression. The following two chapters provide detailed examples of accelerated leadership development in the education sector.

Chapter 6

Accelerated leadership development in schools: Fast-track teachers

- **Fast Track Teaching**
- **Personalising leadership learning**
- **Breaking through the 'concrete ceiling'**
- **Gaps in the research and lessons learned**

Most organisations have staff who have formally, or informally, been recognised as having talent or being the future generation of leaders. Commonly described as 'fast-track' or 'high-potential' employees, these expect, and are expected, to progress speedily through the ranks. This chapter and the next describe initiatives taken by the government to accelerate the leadership development of teachers in schools in England. This chapter outlines the Fast Track Teaching programme and the next describes the Future Leaders programme. The National College has recently commissioned a new accelerated leadership development programme that will offer places for about 200 candidates per annum who will be expected to also gain the National Professional Qualification for Headship (NPQH) and become headteachers within four years. This programme will replace the Fast Track Teaching scheme and will complement the Future Leaders programme. What lessons can be learned from both programmes?

Fast Track Teaching, the focus of this chapter, has many similarities with 'fast streams' within other professions, where individuals with high potential are identified and developed to reach positions of professional influence at an earlier career stage. As shown in Part 1 of this book, accelerated leadership development schemes and programmes exist in many organisations – both private and public – yet little research has been carried out that shows whether accelerated leadership schemes really do:

- attract talent that might otherwise be lost by providing a comparable competitive alternative to private sector and other public sector careers;

- retain talent that would be otherwise lost, motivating the most talented staff by providing them with differentiated challenges to stay;
- enable members of the workforce to reach positions of leadership in a shorter time by ensuring that they are offered enriching professional development opportunities that are less susceptible to variations in work contexts;
- equip workforces to be more effective in those positions by providing targeted training and support through a system of mentoring, coaching and continuing professional development (CPD).

Fast Track Teaching

Established in 2001 by the Department for Education and Skills (DfES), Fast Track was the first accelerated leadership development programme in education in the world. Fast Track was one of several reforms proposed in the 1998 Green Paper, *Teachers: Meeting the challenge of change*, which was intended to modernise the teaching profession. It was devised before the current concern about headteacher recruitment and the demographic 'time bomb' described in the introductory chapter. The idea was to realise the potential of the education system by attracting and motivating school staff through incentives, continuing professional development and support.

To gain entry to the programme, Fast Track teachers completed a selection process that included a behavioural assessment. A core part of the programme involved teachers taking on senior school improvement roles early in their careers in order to provide a wider-school focus. One-to-one coaching was provided, as well as the opportunity to attend residential training targeting interpersonal and intrapersonal development.

In August 2009, when the programme ceased, there were around 2,300 participants, approximately 20 per cent of whom were working in London. Of the total, about one-third (34 per cent) came from the primary sector and 66 per cent from secondary schools. Over half (60 per cent) of participants were under 29 and the vast majority (82 per cent) under 34 years of age. In terms of the ethnic breakdown of participants, this has been consistently in line with the national position, with less than 5 per cent being of ethnic origins other than 'white'.

From an early stage, the programme focused on developing interpersonal skills and intrapersonal capacity within the framework of Northouse's (2004) conceptualisation of leadership and wider business thinking. In part, this was the result of the large numbers of career changers who joined Fast Track from outside the teaching profession and the perspectives that they brought. Having such a substantial number of experienced career changers has resulted not just in learning in relation to supporting career changers in their early years in teaching, but also in significant co-construction of ideas about training between teachers and the programme. This was particularly the case in the early years, when regular focus groups were run in order to design appropriate and sufficiently challenging training.

A significant number of Fast Track courses were designed as part of the programme's provision, among them:

- neuro-linguistic programming (NLP);
- project management;
- consulting skills;
- the use of personality instruments;
- coaching training;
- management skills;
- train the trainer skills;
- leadership training.

Research into the effectiveness of such approaches has provided evidence of positive impact (Jones, 2007; Jones, 2008; Attfield and Jones, 2007a; Attfield, 2007a; Churches and West-Burnham, 2008).

Early access to the NPQH, prior to the redesign of the programme in 2007, has been frequently achieved as a result of the impact of Fast Track teacher 'wider-school focus' work, and research has identified a close synergy and logical progression between the two programmes (Attfield, 2007b). It remains to be seen whether the newly redesigned NPQH will represent such a joined-up 'pipeline' route for the education system's highest flyers, but the new Accelerated Leadership Development (ALD) programme which began in January 2010 sees the NPQH as linking closely. Between October 2002 and April 2007, 135 Fast Trackers joined the NPQH access or development stage. The majority of Fast Track teachers who had achieved access to the NPQH did so in less than three years in teaching. In terms of age, Fast Track teachers had been found to be entering the NPQH, on average, 17 years earlier than their peers (NCSL, 2007a).

In many cases, teachers who are career changers, particularly those with senior experience, have been able to provide insights and a clearer view of processes and challenges within the system. Whether this is the result of their prior leadership experience, or just having a different perspective, is open to debate. However, the provider's experience on Fast Track was that the potential for cross-fertilisation, knowledge and skills transfer between the private and public sectors remains a significantly untapped resource. Furthermore, the integration of areas of learning from applied psychology into Fast Track, including the use of personality instruments as part of development training in communication, conflict and team leadership, remains a largely unique aspect of the programme.

Personalising leadership learning

From its inception, the transference of ideas between business and education has been a fundamental feature of the Fast Track Teaching programme. This has led to a leadership development structure that is more in line with talent management programmes found in industry than the linear, job-title-focused and curriculum-based provision characteristic of much of the old-style leadership provision in education. In many respects, this represents a genuinely personalised approach to leadership learning rather than the complex structuring of layers of differentiated courses, and one focused on the processes (Northouse, 2004) of leadership rather than the content. Drawing on these ideas, Churches and West-Burnham (2008: 8) note that 'it is this focus on the active engagement of the individual that raises the need to explore personal capacity, strategies and skills'. They say that:

> personalising learning requires a focus on the affective dimension as much as any other aspect of organisational life. This is not an area that will change by virtue of policy or mandate – it has to be rooted in personal behaviours.
>
> (Churches and West-Burnham, 2008: 10)

Such views echo the growing recognition of the central importance of interpersonal and intrapersonal skills in both teaching and school leadership (West-Burnham, 2004; West-Burnham and Coates, 2005; West-Burnham and Ireson, 2005), and the relationship between values, behaviour, purpose and school improvement (Leithwood *et al.*, 2006a). Alongside this, CPD is acknowledged to be crucially important in maintaining and enhancing the quality of teaching and learning in schools (e.g. Craft, 2000; Bubb and Earley, 2010); while nationally and internationally, research has shown that: 'where teachers are able to access new ideas and to share ideas more readily, there is a greater potential for school and classroom improvement' (Goodall *et al.*, 2005).

Further, the 'fit' between the development needs of teachers and the selected learning activity is recognised as being critically important in ensuring that there is a positive impact at school and classroom levels (Hopkins *et al.*, 2001). In response to this, as well as ensuring real-life early leadership activity through the 'wider-school focus', the structure of the programme has allowed for individual selection (based on individual needs) from a range of training programmes and one-day training courses aimed at supporting all of the areas above. Table 6.1 illustrates some of the training options made available to participants of the Fast Track programme.

Table 6.1: Examples of Fast Track training options

• Behaviour management – the structure, attitude and skills of excellence • Change management • Dealing with parents and stakeholders • Effective school self-evaluation • Establishing your first management role • Everyone matters – making Every Child Matters and Wellbeing a reality • The learning classroom • Understanding self and others using FIRO-B® • Wider school focus – sharing best practice and moving towards senior management • Young Gifted and Talented	• Authentic leadership (an exploration of being yourself) [including personality feedback] • Coaching for leadership • Consulting and influencing skills for leaders – Level 1 • Consulting and influencing skills for leaders – Level 2 • Creative thinking skills for leadership • Leading and influencing groups • Life–balance excellence • Making it happen • Management skills in schools • NLP for Teachers and School Leaders – Level 1 • NLP for Teachers and School Leaders – Level 2 • Project management • Train the trainer (an accelerated learning course)

Ideas about personalising leadership learning have been included in Fast Track training since 2004, and these ideas have filtered down into the programme's structure as well as into the learning of Fast Track teachers. Consequently, from an early stage, the programme has had an innovative personalised learning structure. This structure is also found in the redesigned NPQH programme – although much less emphasis is given to 'training courses' (Crawford and Earley, 2010).

The Fast Track programme has no accreditation and participants are not required to follow a specific route or curriculum. Participants have been largely free to choose training and development opportunities from a personalised perspective rather than a differentiated one. This reflects the programme's presentation of leadership development as a 'mosaic' of self-development and experience rather than a linear journey with traditional accreditation points and stages. Targeting professional development and support more effectively, through personalised learning approaches, has allowed the programme to maintain quality and impact while continuing to meet the needs of an increasingly differentiated group of learners (Jones, 2007; Attfield and Jones, 2007b).

A research study that looked at the impact of CPD on the leadership development of Fast Track teachers, using Guskey's (2000) five levels of evaluation as a framework, found that:

> *Targeting professional development and support more effectively, through personalised learning approaches, has allowed the programme to maintain quality and impact whilst continuing to meet the needs of an increasingly differentiated group of learners.*
>
> (Jones, 2007: 5)

At the heart of this attempt to conceptualise the leadership learning journey was the idea of the development of an understanding of self within a framework of learning created by the Fast Track teachers themselves. To support this process, Fast Track teachers had regular leadership coaching which was structured around the GROW model (Whitmore, 2003) allowing for a focus on the development of self first. Aligned with this, a central feature of the programme was the 'wider school focus' through which all participants take on a significant whole-school responsibility early in their career. This provides real-life leadership learning and experience of the interpersonal and intrapersonal challenges that may need to be encountered in order to achieve effective early leadership development (Attfield and Jones, 2007a; Jones, 2007). This approach aimed to ensure that participants have already experienced and overcome significant organisational leadership challenges before being appointed to a formal senior leadership role.

Feedback from Fast Track teachers and analysis of data suggest that the wider school focus was a significant factor in the achievement of rapid succession to senior posts and progression to the NPQH. In total, 24,232 field reports on Fast Track teacher progress have been recorded since the start of the programme. These contain not only biometric and progression data but also qualitative reports on the contexts, challenges faced and the activities of Fast Track teachers. Data and information were processed on a regular basis and have been one of the principal means by which common themes and research and development issues have emerged and been identified. Analysis of reports suggests that taking on an early wider school, or whole-school, leadership responsibility appears to help in the development of a range of skills and competencies, and may give the sort of real-life experiences that help high-flying leaders to develop. As noted in Chapter 5 (Table 5.2), McCall (1998) identified 16 developmental experiences that can have a key influence on their rate and level of development.

Breaking through the 'concrete ceiling': Progression, impact and development

The National College review of the Fast Track programme concluded that:

> *Overall, Fast Track has been a success. There is evidence that those on the programme have taken on comparatively more responsibility, gained more teaching and learning responsibility (TLR) payments… Over 200 teachers have graduated from the programme and the growth in the number of Fast Track alumni is beginning to accelerate. Teachers who have been on Fast Track consistently exhibit more leadership, management and transformational behaviours in schools.*
>
> (Jones, 2008: 5)

However, since the publication of this report in 2008, the number of Fast Track teachers who have gained early promotion to an assistant headship, deputy headship, headship or LA advisory post has significantly increased from 176 (Jones, 2008: 9) to 295 (NCSL, 2008b). The suggestion here is that a critical 'tipping point' of success may have been reached in relation to the approach and impact of the programme. Sixty per cent of Fast Track Teaching alumni were under 30 at the time of their promotion and 86 per cent were under 39. In addition, the Jones review (2008) limited itself to the analysis of progression against national Teaching and Learning Responsibility (TLR1 and TLR2) data. Recent figures published by NCSL (2008a) demonstrate clearly the significant contribution that Fast Track teaching has made, when compared to national statistics on the number of teachers who achieve promotion to Leadership Group Pay Spine posts in years 0–4 and 5–9.

The continued need to engage specifically with young, talented school leaders, very early in their careers, is clearly indicated in the national statistics that show that in 2004 (DfES, 2004) only 0.07 per cent of male teachers in years 0–4 of teaching were in a Leadership Group Pay Spine post in secondary schools; and that in primary schools the percentage was only 0.3 per cent. The figures for female teachers are even more dramatic and show that in 2004 only 0.03 per cent of female teachers in years 0–4 were in a Leadership Group Pay Spine post in secondary schools, and that in primary schools the percentage was only 0.05 per cent.

Cumulative percentages for teachers in years 0–9 show that only 0.7 per cent of male teachers in years 0–9 of teaching were in a Leadership Group Pay Spine post in secondary schools and that in primary schools the percentage was only 4.06 per cent; and that only 1.8 per cent of female teachers in years 0–9 were in a Leadership Group Pay Spine post in secondary schools and that in primary schools the percentage was only 0.4 per cent.

Figures for 2006 (which include around 100 Fast Track alumni) show only limited or no improvement, depending on group (DfES, 2006). However, Fast Track teacher progression over the period 2004–08 has increased significantly in terms of both progression in years 0–4 and in years 0–9. In particular, in 2004, there were nationally only 260 female teachers in a Leadership Group Pay Spine post in years 0–4. As of October 2008, 173 female Fast Track teachers have achieved such a promotion – the vast majority of whom achieved this in years 3–5 of teaching.

The rate of progression against the national trend is perhaps most dramatically illustrated in relation to female teacher progression. In relation to overall demographics, 70 per cent of Fast Track teachers are female.

Gaps in the research and lessons learned

Overall, what seems to have made the difference is that Fast Track has provided:

- an opportunity for teachers to learn to lead with a genuine school strategic leadership task;
- interpersonal and intrapersonal training to support development gaps identified through an applied psychology approach;
- a context around the Fast Track teacher and the mindsets of the headteacher in the school;
- the application of sustained and well-funded support to ensure face-to-face learning opportunities;
- extensive support for women to help them in overcoming the 'concrete ceiling'.

That said, a fundamental question for any government intent on pursuing a future accelerated leadership development programme within the public sector has to be one of financial commitment and cost. As the formal NCSL evaluation of the programme noted:

> Fast Track has not been without its problems, not least the speed with which it outgrew available funding. This led to some difficult decisions having to be taken on how to provide professional development for large numbers of teachers who had raised expectations of the programme provision. Annual budgets grew by 55 per cent between 2003/04 and 2006/07, at a time when Fast Track teacher numbers grew by at least 142 per cent. As numbers grew, the support provided had to be reduced to a point where the impact of Fast Track was adversely affected. Over the last 18–24 months of the programme, before the announcement was made that recruitment to Fast Track was to end, the level of resources committed had been insufficient to sustain the

early achievements. Growing numbers of teachers had become less satisfied with the professional development (PD) achieved through the programme, and the progress made by Fast Track in schools was beginning to be eroded.

(Jones, 2008)

The programme's critics rightly point out its high cost and they raise the issue about whether a system should spend so much on identified individuals when there is little or no guarantee that they will become senior leaders or heads.

Beyond the simple resource issues raised above, there is the question of long-term commitment and the nature of support for the most talented. Research commissioned by CfBT Education Trust demonstrated that the labour market was having a substantial influence on Fast Track teacher progression (Howson, 2007b). In relation to the secondary school context it concluded that:

Our view is that the secondary sector has sufficient candidates for headship and that recent difficulties have been due to temporary reductions in supply caused by factors such as the introduction of the assistant head grade in 2000 and the introduction of a compulsory NPQH requirement for first-time heads in 2004.

(Howson, 2007b: 14)

In relation to Fast Track, the report recommended the development of a

service to draw Fast Track graduates to jobs that meet their requirements…such a scheme would also provide management information about areas where candidates were finding it difficult to secure promotion or, conversely, where schools had little choice of candidates from the Fast Track programme.

(Howson, 2007b: 43)

Overall, the number of entry-level senior leadership posts being created by schools is less than would probably be necessary to ensure rapid progress through a job title promotion-based system. Consequently, teachers seeking progression find themselves having to make significant re-locations in order to make progress. These factors should be taken into account in any decisions about future accelerated leadership support. In addition, data about the number of years in teaching and speed of progression suggest that accelerated development should be supported over timescales greater than five years, rather than less than five years, if the maximum return on investment is to be achieved, particularly for those who join leadership programmes from outside the profession and who will need a reasonable period of professional embedding. What the data suggest is that even with such an initial period, progression is much more rapid than for the general teacher population when approaches such as those on Fast Track are applied.

Fast Track remains unique and, in many ways, in opposition to the traditional job-related, skills-based, approaches to leadership development in education. In the light of the most recent statistics, and the wealth of both qualitative and quantitative research data that are held within the programme, a substantial research programme should, in our view, have been undertaken before any significant changes to the programme structure and delivery were made – particularly bearing in mind the apparent 'tipping point' that may have been reached. Furthermore, if Fast Track has been an experiment in anything then having a behavioural assessment centre has made it an experiment in the identification of future leaders according to behavioural criteria. Significantly, recent research (Leithwood *et al.*, 2006a; Day *et al.*, 2009) has suggested that a small handful of personal traits explain a high proportion of the variation in leadership effectiveness.

> [E]vidence warrants the claim that, at least under challenging circumstances, the most successful school leaders are open-minded and ready to learn from others. They are also flexible rather than dogmatic in their thinking within a system of core values, persistent (e.g. in pursuit of high expectations of staff motivation, commitment, learning and achievement for all), resilient and optimistic. Such traits help explain why successful leaders facing daunting conditions are often able to push forward when there is little reason to expect progress.
>
> (Leithwood *et al.*, 2006a: 14)

Furthermore, the Jones review recommended that 'There is a need for any future selection process, for the proposed accelerated leadership provision, to reflect the experience of Fast Track in employing rigorous and robust selection' (2008: 6). This is a recommendation that has been taken on board by both the new, revised and more personalised NPQH (Crawford and Earley, 2010) and the Future Leaders programme, the subject of the next chapter.

Summary

The introduction of the Fast Track programme was a bold move on the part of the national government in England, but it has now ceased to operate and has been subsumed and reconfigured, along with Future Leaders, within the National College's *Accelerate to Headship* programmes.

Chapter 7

Accelerated leadership development in schools: Future Leaders

- **Future Leaders**
- **The programme**
- **Phases of the programme**
- **Perceived impact**

The second fast-track educational leadership programme, Future Leaders, aims to develop both practising teachers and high-quality individuals currently not in the schools teaching system who would like to become heads, deputy heads and assistant heads in urban secondary schools. The programme was created in response to the shortage of teachers taking on senior roles within schools, which is particularly acute in urban areas. It also aims to create a cadre of school leaders who commit their future careers to working in challenging urban secondary schools.

Future Leaders

The scheme is managed by Future Leaders with support from the National College for Leadership of Schools and Children's Services, Absolute Return for Kids (ARK), the (then) Department for Children, Schools and Families (DCSF) and the Specialist Schools and Academies Trust (SSAT). The idea is based on the New Leaders for New Schools (NLNS) programme in New York. This is a US non-profit organisation which is founded on five core beliefs and selects and trains individuals from within education, as well as former educators, to become urban school principals. It calls itself 'a movement to transform urban schools nationally and locally' and has financial support from the Bill and Melinda Gates Foundation and the Broad Foundation. In 2001, NLNS began to train a cohort of 13 people in New York City and Chicago. Since then, the total number of New Leaders has grown to 427 school leaders in 2007. About one new city partnership has been formed each year – Oakland in 2002, Washington, DC in 2003, Memphis in 2004, Baltimore in 2005, Milwaukee in 2006, and both Prince George's County, Maryland and New Orleans in 2007.

In January 2006, a group from the (then) NCSL, ARK and SSAT visited New York for a five-day feasibility study. They saw how NLNS worked in New York and Maryland and visited several charter schools. On returning to London, individuals from NCSL, SSAT and ARK planned the Future Leaders training programme, using the NLNS model as a starting point. The feasibility report was written and the group met government ministers in early March 2006. Full approval for the scheme was obtained in late March.

The objectives of the Future Leaders programme are as follows:

- Expand the pool from which headteachers can be found for urban complex schools.
- Recruit from non-traditional sources.
- Provide a model for culture change by changing attitudes to recruitment of senior staff in schools.
- Provide an alternative approach for teachers and those not currently in schools to gain a fast track to senior roles (headships) in a shorter time span.

The programme was initially offered in London in 2006 to 20 participants. New cohorts of 20–30 teachers started each year from 2007 to 2009. It was expanded to Manchester in 2008 and a year later to the Black Country in the West Midlands. Currently the Future Leaders programme has scaled up to a total of over 150 participants in three large cities in England.

The programme

All those involved in the pilot had previously held a teaching position in schools, and qualified teacher status (QTS) was required for them to be part of this fast-track leadership development programme. After selection and summer training at the National College in Nottingham, each participant undertook a one-year full-time placement with a host school where the Future Leader (FL) joined the senior leadership team (SLT). They were mentored by the school head and coached by one of four external coaches, all of whom had been successful heads of urban schools. Towards the end of the first year, the participants applied for posts as deputy head or assistant head within a secondary school, which they would take up in their second year, during which time they would continue to receive support.

Four main phases of the programme can therefore be identified:

1. Recruitment, assessment and selection;
2. Training – foundation and ongoing;
3. Experience for a year in the host school;
4. Employment as a senior leader.

The phases of the pilot programme were evaluated over the first two years and this chapter draws upon the main findings of the evaluation (Earley *et al.*, 2008). In the first year the focus was on assessment and the programme. Questions asked included the following:

The assessment process that identifies the participants:

- How robust is the recruitment process?
- Is it successful in identifying those participants who best meet the criteria for participation on the programme?
- Does it prepare participants for the programme?

The FL programme:

- How far is the programme achieving its aims and objectives?
- To what extent is the programme meeting the needs of the participants?
- To what extent do the participants feel prepared for Year Two of the programme?

The main focus of the second year of the evaluation was two-fold:

- To assess the impact of the programme as pilot participants (FL1) moved to senior leadership positions in secondary schools.
- To monitor the development of the programme with the second cohort of participants (FL2).

The evaluation looked at all the phases and included undertaking school visits to gather information about the Future Leaders' experiences in the host schools. Methods for collecting data for the evaluation included a questionnaire survey, interviews (both face-to-face and telephone) of Future Leaders and other key stakeholders, and attending/observing events. Each of the phases of the programme is briefly considered in turn.

Phases of the programme

Phase 1: Recruitment, assessment and selection

The initial cohort of 20 participants involved in the pilot was drawn from a pool of 190 potential candidates. The application and selection process was quite complex and included several stages – an application form, an essay question, online exercises (a picture story exercise and a personal values questionnaire), interviews and participation in an assessment centre. For the candidates who successfully completed the initial stages, these were followed by an initial 'behavioural event' interview. The behavioural event interview required applicants to think about whether they really could be a leader in a complex urban school. Feedback was given on the interview and its usefulness as a preparation for the assessment day. During the assessment day, which involved over 40 applicants, they were exposed to a variety of tasks and undertook a number of activities including role plays, case studies, a coaching video lesson and a reflective interview conducted by a London headteacher.

As part of the evaluation, questionnaire responses were received from 45 per cent of the 190 applicants to the programme (a higher percentage was returned from those who were offered a place and a lower percentage from those who only reached the first stage of the assessment process). The main reasons given for applicants' initial attraction to Future Leaders were: the focus on challenging urban schools (60 per cent); the fact that it was an 'innovative programme' (45 per cent); and the programme's 'strong mission and beliefs' (32 per cent). The fact that it was London-based was an attraction for 26 per cent, while 18 per cent cited the opportunity to get back into teaching at a senior level as a reason for applying. Interestingly, over one-third noted 'the speed of getting to senior leadership' (37 per cent) as the main reason for applying.

When asked what attracted them to urban education, a number of key themes emerged, including the 'challenge' of working in these settings. Alongside the challenge there was also a strong commitment to social justice and equity and providing opportunities for disadvantaged children. Another strong theme was that they themselves had come from such a background and understood the importance of education as a way out of disadvantage. A further reason was a 'service' orientation – that is, that they felt a duty or sense of responsibility towards children in urban schools.

The majority of candidates were positive about all the aspects of the assessment day, although one or two who were not offered a place reacted against it. The one aspect that some candidates thought might enhance the selection process would be the opportunity to interact in some way with some 'real students', or to demonstrate their teaching ability. Perhaps not surprisingly, those who had gone through the whole process and had been selected tended to be the most positive about the organisation and value of it. Interestingly, half of all those who did not make the final selection said they would consider applying again. The process of selecting candidates for the second cohort was changed in the light of feedback. In 2007, the selection process was streamlined and currently includes the observation of the applicants teaching a lesson.

Phase 2: Foundation and ongoing training

The foundation training includes two weekend sessions in the summer term followed by a two-week residential course in the summer holidays. Participants greatly enjoyed the intensity and pace. They described it as 'very impressive', 'refreshingly challenging' and 'inspirational and aspirational'. The training was very good for bonding the group together and working with the coaches. They particularly liked hearing headteachers talk about their experience of headship: 'So it wasn't theory, it was really happening in school'.

The training experience included a trip to schools in New York or Boston led by principals from NLNS, which the participants valued greatly. A person from the resident school, usually the head, also went on the trip, and participants greatly valued the time for discussion. However, a few of the heads were less impressed than the Future Leaders with what they saw in the schools.

The training continued with weekly afternoon sessions, which were generally deemed to be of high quality and to bring people together. However, some participants found them hard to attend because of the demands of their role in school.

Phase 3: Experience in the host school (residency)

The initial experience of the Future Leaders in their resident schools was generally perceived to have been good ('very welcoming', 'very positive'), but shaped by the headteacher and the school's culture. Two used the phrase 'hit the ground running' to explain their initial experiences (one stated that because of the training received she was able to do this successfully), but another noted that the first days were awful as she felt completely out of her 'comfort zone'.

Nomenclature was important too and Future Leaders were introduced as Associate Heads, Associate Deputies, Trainee Deputies or Assistant Heads. Future Leaders had suggested that they were referred to as Associate Deputy Heads, but clearly schools had their own preferences.

The reactions to senior staff from the Future Leaders was very positive, with comments like 'brilliant', 'fantastic', 'very welcoming and supportive' quite common. Where there was any qualification it was usually with reference to a single SLT member whose reaction had been problematic. Three Future Leaders cited difficulties where the deputy saw them 'as a challenge' or was 'less accepting', but in most cases this had been resolved once their worth had been demonstrated. One spoke of an age divide that had been reflected in the team's reaction to her arrival:

The reaction of the senior staff has been funny. The deputies, all older and more experienced, have taken me under their wing but not in a patronising way – so they've reacted very well, they've been encouraging and kind. I share an office with one of them. The Assistant Heads are all younger (early 30s), they're very career minded and have worked for [the head] for many years – most came with him from his previous school in [name of LA]. I sense a little bit more hostility from them – 'who does she think she is', and so on!

Perhaps this comment sums up the situation best:

It's been fine. I thought it might be more difficult than it has been but they've all accepted me so no problem at all.

Reactions from staff, like their senior colleagues, had generally been positive and very welcoming. In one case there was a degree of wariness from a head of department (in the same subject area as the Future Leader's) but this had been resolved. Future Leaders spoke of how well the head had prepared the ground and how they (the FLs) had been very careful to act professionally and prove their worth. For example, there was a fight in the playground, which the Future Leader and the deputy had dealt with. Later, staff told the FL that they had been watching her and were impressed with how she had followed it up. Credibility was also earned with staff through good classroom practices.

A central part of the residency was the mentoring provided by the head. Each participant, as part of their support during their period in the host school, had an external coach and mentoring from the head. Headteachers were expected to meet with the Future Leaders on a regular basis, but this was not always happening. How useful the sessions with the head were proved to be varied. Nearly half of the Future Leaders used positive phrases like 'very useful' ('it makes all the difference') or 'it's essential' or 'it's been incredibly constructive', but for one the jury was still out ('call me back in a year!'). Clearly the role of the headteacher is crucially important and will affect the success of the scheme. A challenge for the Future Leaders scheme is to increase the stock of 'good' placement schools.

Each participant was also assigned to a coach, who was independent of the school and who had been a headteacher. For cohorts 1 and 2 there were four coaches working with the participants. The coach was the key link between the skills taught in the Foundation courses and the integration of these skills into practice by the residents. The coach supported their personal and professional development and gave feedback on the Future Leader's progress. Coaches regularly visited the participants in their schools and generally had a one-to-one session with them. They also talked to the heads about the Future Leader's performance and whether there were any issues that needed to be addressed. Overall, the coaches were seen very positively by the participants and had given useful feedback and support during their entry into school and in their ongoing involvement with their schools. Participants appreciated the availability of someone with headship experience to talk things through with and bounce ideas off. During the second year, while they valued the support, participants wanted more 'pressure' from the coaches.

As part of the 'residency' the Future Leaders are encouraged to consider with their coach 22 Units under the following five headings.

1. Shaping the future of an urban complex school;
2. Leading the learning in an urban complex school;
3. Managing an urban complex school;
4. Securing accountability in an urban complex school;
5. Developing the urban community.

The second cohort of Future Leaders has also had structured support from a deputy acting in the role of 'professional tutor' (PT). This has been very successful in about a third of cases. However, problems centred around the PT not having time or the inclination to do the role, not having the skills or not understanding what was needed. In some cases the Future Leaders met rarely with their PT, did not receive any professional tutoring or have anything other than line management meetings.

When asked how well they thought they had done in school, the majority of Future Leaders were positive about their achievements (e.g. 'good feedback so far', 'glowing praise from the head') but several included caveats and qualifications (e.g. 'doing well but it's an easy place to do a good job', 'OK but just OK', 'hard to say – fine', 'so far so good').

When participants were asked what had been the most difficult thing so far, the answers were wide-ranging. In some cases they reflected the particular Future Leader's circumstances (e.g. split-site school, being a single parent, doing two jobs, lesson planning, heavy teaching load) but reference was also made to time management, workload/work–life balance, fitting into the school's ethos, dealing with staff, and the challenge of getting a job for next September. Also, two participants made reference to the difficulty of moving from a middle manager/leader role to one of senior leadership.

Most of the Future Leaders had no doubt that they had become more effective leaders because of the programme, and the vast majority said they had no regrets about joining the scheme, but some were anxious about getting a job after the placement. In this fast-track programme, Future Leaders are required to give up their posts rather than be seconded from them, as is the case with some other schemes. Most of the participants said that Future Leaders was really exciting.

Phase 4: Employment as a senior leader

Towards the end of their residency year, the programme participants apply for substantive posts as deputies or assistant heads. The destinations of the first cohort varied in terms of their postings, and this was even more evident for the second cohort. The post obtained had a huge influence on their future plans and expectations for reaching headship. Table 7.1 compares the posts of the two groups.

Table 7.1: Destination posts of Future Leader cohorts 1 and 2 at the end of their one-year residency

Post	Cohort 1	Cohort 2
Permanent deputy headship	13	8
Temporary deputy headship	3	3
Permanent assistant headship	3	6
Temporary assistant headship	0	6
Extension of residency period	0	4
Other (e.g. consultancy)	0	1
No post by September	0	1
Totals	19	29

The 13 people from cohort 1 in permanent deputy posts expected to gain a headship for 2009/10. Of the 29 members of the second cohort, just under a half (14) obtained permanent posts. Of these, eight were at deputy-head level and six at assistant-head level. Four of those who secured substantive posts did so within their residency schools. In fact, over one-third (11) of cohort 2 continued working in their residency school in some capacity during the following school year.

On balance, it appears that in both cohorts there was a mix of ability and experience among those selected, which led to a broader range of outcomes than might be expected. Overall, people in cohort 2 were less successful in obtaining substantive posts following the residency, due to a number of factors. The coaches and some heads expressed the view that the selection process for this group was not as robust as for the first cohort, and that this led to some unsuitable people being accepted onto the course. There were some older candidates who struggled to find suitable positions. Most, however, were expected to achieve headship eventually, if not within four years.

By 2009, 94 per cent of those who had completed their residency year were in senior leadership team positions and four Future Leaders had been appointed headteachers, after only three years on the programme.

Perceived impact

The Future Leaders perceived their impact to be on a range of aspects of school activity such as behaviour, attendance, student voice, raising the attainment levels of teaching groups, sustaining the performance of departments, undertaking professional development with colleagues, analysis of exam data, and creating a thoughtful, reflective approach among the staff. Nine of cohort 1 were said by the heads to have had 'high impact', five 'medium to high impact', two had 'some impact' and only one was seen as having 'no impact'. Both cohorts were asked what they perceived to be the factors that hindered the impact they were having in their schools. The following factors were noted:

- not being given enough responsibility during the residency;
- distraction with job applications;
- the managerial leadership style of the head, who did not delegate or build capacity;
- schools not knowing what to do with the FL in terms of role and responsibility;
- not feeling fully accepted by the SLT or other teachers;
- allocated teaching in areas where they had no experience;
- SLT who did not share the same vision/goals as the Future Leaders mission;
- lack of self-confidence.

There was common agreement across the various participants about the benefits of the programme, which were seen as the training, the coaching, the networking and support from the other Future Leaders, the vision of the programme, and the reflection and adaptation by the Future Leaders organisation. Residency school heads made positive reference to the external perspectives, different ways of working, extra capacity and the introduction of new ideas that the Future Leaders brought into the schools. Some heads noted that the impact the participants were having was in some cases considerable and they welcomed many of their attributes and abilities.

While the first year of the pilot scheme was seen by all those involved as a considerable success, the responses to the second year were more mixed. The scheme depends for its success on a complex interplay of three major components: the residency school (and specifically the head and professional tutor); the Future Leader themselves; and the support offered by the coaches and the Future Leaders organisation. In most cases during the first year of the pilot this worked very well. In the second year the evaluators found that the picture was patchier and that some Future Leaders were not significantly benefiting from their placements.

Interestingly, there is no evidence from the evaluations of either Future Leaders or Fast Track teachers causing resentment or hostility on the part of those not involved. One of the unintended consequences of the Future Leaders programme, for example, is that some individuals not on the programme look at themselves in a new light, perhaps seeing themselves as equally capable as the selected high-potential participant. What seemed to matter most in both ALD programmes was the ability of the selected participants to do the job and to demonstrate their credibility in the classroom and in the school.

The National College's 'Evidence into Practice Guide' *What are we learning about…identifying talent?* (NCSL, 2009a) draws upon the experience of the two ALD programmes discussed in Chapters 6 and 7 in order to offer pointers as to what works best as well as pitfalls to avoid. A checklist for local talent development planning was devised and this was summarised in Chapter 3.

Summary

The future looks positive for the Future Leaders scheme, an initiative, it will be recalled, that had its origins in the USA with New Leaders for New Schools. Some of the Future Leaders spoke of belonging to or having signed up to 'the movement'; it appears as though the movement is beginning to take off and it has been allocated funding to continue operating in London and other urban conurbations. Indeed, in 2009 the National College launched the Accelerate to Headship programme, which has two accelerated routes: 'Tomorrow's Heads' and 'Future Leaders'. Future Leaders is now part of the Accelerate to Headship programme aimed at current or former teachers who are committed to leading a challenging urban secondary school in London, the North West, the West Midlands or the Humber.

The next chapter offers further pointers to good practice and asks what schools should consider if they wish to implement an ALD programme.

Chapter 8

A fast-track leadership development strategy for schools

- **Customising an ALD strategy**
- **Six considerations**
- **Leadership development survey**

The previous two chapters described national accelerated leadership development (ALD) programmes – one now disbanded and the other subsumed as part of the new Accelerate to Headship programme – but it is unlikely that reliance on centrally administered programmes will be sufficient to meet the number of senior school leaders needed in the future. As the National College (NCSL, 2008b: 9) has argued, 'we need to become much better at identifying potential leaders and finding ways to accelerate their development at the school and local level'.

Whereas most public and private organisations appear to have established their own ALD methods, schools may find it more difficult – even undesirable – to set up on their own. Schools wishing to develop a bespoke model of accelerated development are of course free to do so. Others, because of their size, staffing profile, scale of challenge, or financial considerations, may prefer to work in partnerships such as clusters, networks or collaboratives. Furthermore, others might prefer to rely more on the support and facilitation provided by their respective local authorities. One thing is crucial, however, and that is that the initiative should be led and co-ordinated by highly competent senior leaders who have the skills, commitment, credibility and respect of colleagues.

The focus of this chapter is on best practices associated with ALD programmes, including the initial identification and management of high-potential staff. It proposes 'six considerations' or a model for schools that helps them develop support structures and systems to make the right choices. Governors, headteachers, members of senior leadership teams, school finance officers, and others from outside the school – for example officers from local authorities, or diocesan boards – should all find relevance in the content of this chapter for their respective strategic roles. This chapter offers a systematic process for introducing ALD programmes and attempts to predict the kinds of considerations schools might need to take into account in developing their strategy.

Customising an ALD strategy

Although leadership succession is a national issue, there is general agreement that it requires a 'local solutions' approach. One option available to schools, working in collaboration with other stakeholders, is to identify high-potential talent from their own ranks and accelerate their progression to senior posts – a popular and successful practice in a range of public and private sector organisations. Not only will this strategy help address the impending shortfall in senior school leaders but it will also improve retention rates and send a strong message about the qualities that are valued. The key thing is to identify the right people from within the organisation and to provide them with a range of high-level experiences and opportunities.

In Chapter 2 we examined some of the characteristics and features of talented and high-potential individuals. Based on an online survey of heads, the Hay Group (2008) suggests that 'early warning signs for leadership potential' include:

- confidence and credibility;
- the ability to see the big picture, to make connections and think of the whole school;
- mastering the basics of the role quickly and looking for more;
- getting involved (doesn't look the other way or walk past incidents);
- initiative and self-motivation (the sort of people you can't stop from leading);
- intellectual curiosity and capacity (sees the common threads);
- resilience and empathy (to survive the pace of acceleration and learn from others).

Interestingly, the same survey found that high-performing schools were five times more likely than other schools to have processes in place for identifying leadership potential.

Barnes (2008: 5) notes that the senior leaders in his study expected potential leaders to be high-quality classroom practitioners and, inter alia, to be strong in relationships with others, to meet deadlines, to be willing to learn and request training, and to contribute to meetings and discussions.

Six considerations

Consideration 1: Why should we try to accelerate leadership development?

Many schools are finding it difficult to recruit leaders. This problem is not confined to schools, since there appears to be a scarcity of leadership talent in all sectors, globally. However, in order to achieve the best outcomes for all children and young people, we must ensure that we have enough talented people willing to take up leadership positions in our schools. One way to achieve this is to work in partnership with other local schools, the local authority, the diocese, higher education institutions, and other public and private sector organisations to grow the next generation of school leaders by accelerating the leadership development of staff.

Experience from other sectors shows that this approach has led to significant success. For example, Pepsico, 3M, and Rolls Royce select the best-performing managers for specialised leadership development programmes. Staff are selected on the basis of their potential to become future leaders of the business. The focus is on finding those people capable of *building* the business rather than merely *running* the business, which is regarded as a manager's job.

As shown in the previous two chapters, the Fast Track Teaching and Future Leaders programmes have both illustrated that talented staff can be accelerated to senior leadership roles in 3–4 years – sometimes even less – if successfully mentored, coached and provided with high-quality development opportunities. In business and industry, although practice varies from sector to sector, it is possible to achieve senior status relatively quickly, for example in 12 to 18 months. Fujitsu is an example of a company that set up an intensive 12-month fast-track development programme to support and develop individuals so that they could fill a specific managerial post.

Consideration 2: Do we need to accelerate the leadership development of staff?

Before you can answer this question with any degree of confidence, you may need to gather relevant local data on this issue.

THINGS TO DO 1

Ask the relevant person in your school or local authority administration team to provide you with details of your school's projected retirements. A tool that enables local authorities to gather area data can be found at: www.nationalcollege.org.uk/tomorrowsleaderstoday

To help, we have provided you with a brief and straightforward exercise for your own personal reference or to use at a meeting of a group of appropriate colleagues to help you highlight the main succession planning issues for the school.

Does your school have sufficient leadership strength to staff its growth and its improvement plans?	Yes	No
What is the reason for your answer?		

Has the organisation experienced a long-term vacancy in a key leadership position in the last year?	Yes	No
What is the reason for your answer?		

Did/will you have to go outside the organisation to fill the position?	Yes	No
What is the reason for your answer?		

What is/will be the cost to the school of recruiting externally?
What is the reason for your answer?

Has the school had to compromise on leadership quality to fill certain leadership positions?	Yes	No
What is the reason for your answer?		

What percentage of your leaders would be selected if they were applying today for their current positions?
What is the reason for your answer?

Have the leadership challenges faced by your senior leaders changed significantly during the past 5–10 years?	Yes	No
What is the reason for your answer?		

Would your senior leaders say that they felt adequately prepared for their roles when they first took them on?	Yes	No
What is the reason for your answer?		

Do many people who are ready or are being groomed for promotion typically leave the school before they get that promotion?	Yes	No
What is the reason for your answer?		

Consideration 3: What would acceleration mean for us?

<u>Cost and timescale</u>

Establishing a strategy for accelerating leadership development is not without its costs – both in terms of finance and time. However, to gain a full picture, the costs incurred in setting up and maintaining a strategy should be compared with those that might well be incurred in establishing a full recruitment and selection process. Such a process would involve advertisement costs, the travel and accommodation costs of candidates, the time of governors and others involved in the selection, etc. Anecdotal evidence indicates that these costs can amount to many thousands of pounds.

<u>Identifying talented staff for acceleration</u>

Identifying the right people for acceleration is essential. They need to be individuals who are most likely to strengthen the organisation's leadership capacity – and thus, its future. Make every effort to ensure that the identification process is:

- accurate;
- efficient;
- fair.

There are several actions that can ensure that a wide range of people is considered:

THINGS TO DO 2

- Create a list of all staff who meet the organisation's minimum requirements.
- Create another list of staff who have undertaken activities or in other ways have attracted positive attention.
- Ask line managers and other appropriate colleagues for recommendations from within their departments and areas.
- List people who have indicated an interest in senior leadership when completing their performance reviews or when appointed.
- Take soundings from local authority personnel and others who work closely with staff in your school.

<u>Drawing up selection criteria</u>

Research findings, from a variety of settings – both private and public sector – tell us that talented staff display not only a range of general characteristics but also more specific learning, attitudinal and behavioural ones. Some of these are set out in Table 8.1.

Table 8.1: General and psychological characteristics displayed by talented staff

General characteristics	Psychological characteristics
High-potential staff: • have a unique perception of their job; • demonstrate a broad thinking style; • have an awareness of time; • value independence and self-responsibility; • show high commitment and high energy; • are creative and enjoy variety; • have a varying interest in teamwork; • seek continual improvement.	High-potential staff: • see work as a primary source of satisfaction; • are able to stretch time and energy if managed well; • regard problems as opportunities; • are interested in their career development; • value regular and systematic feedback; • reflect upon and capture their learning; • seek personal and professional fulfilment in their job.
Motivational characteristics	*Learning characteristics*
High-potential staff: • see new initiatives positively; • have a strong work ethic and enjoy working hard; • enjoy being dominant and having influence; • strive for excellence; • have a concern with status; • need challenge; • need regular new tasks; • seek opportunities for career development; • respond well to clear values and direction; • seek roles that allow them to be fulfilled.	High-potential staff: • learn quickly; • integrate new information to direct future activity; • adapt to new situations; • develop high levels of job-specific knowledge; • have an orientation towards learning from others; • take risks in their development and work; • respond to feedback; • learn from mistakes; • are open to criticism.

> **THINGS TO DO 3**
>
> Working individually (e.g. CPD leader, talent manager) or in teams (e.g. senior leadership team, talent development team, CPD team), try to apply the characteristics set out above to those on your staff who show high potential.
>
> How secure is the evidence upon which you base your views?

Managing the process

> **THINGS TO DO 4**
>
> Think about the school's management structure and judge whether the role of 'talent manager' is currently being performed by anyone, e.g. a member of the senior leadership team, CPD Leader.
>
> How content are you with the nature of the role and how well it is being performed?
>
> If the role is not allocated currently, what plans do you have to do so?
>
> Is there scope and benefit for the role to be carried out across a network or cluster of schools?
>
> How are the views of governors and other stakeholders gathered and considered?

Consideration 4: How might we provide acceleration opportunities?

Accelerated development opportunities

Although many organisations, such as Honda and the National Health Service, invest heavily in talent management, others, such as Abbey and Surrey County Council, look for low-cost, even no-cost, development opportunities for their staff. Increasingly, organisations are concentrating their efforts on development activities that have proven value but which cost relatively little, for example networking, mentoring and coaching. The following is a non-exhaustive list of opportunities that might be provided for staff to help them accelerate their leadership development:

- solving a difficult problem;
- assuming a significant leadership role;
- building and leading a team;
- following through with a plan, product, process, etc.;
- managing a partnership opportunity;
- implementing a school-wide change;
- handling an emergency situation;
- learning and applying skills quickly;

- dealing with conflict, change, or hurt feelings;
- identifying and selecting staff;
- undertaking productive performance management reviews;
- leading a team through personal influence;
- overseeing a school-based process;
- negotiating agreements with external organisations;
- dealing with people from different disciplines, cultures or with diverse perspectives;
- operating in high-pressure or high-visibility situations;
- making presentations to senior leaders in schools, local authorities, business;
- controlling costs against a fixed budget.

THINGS TO DO 5

How do you currently present leadership development opportunities for staff in your school?

Draw up a list of activities, tasks, opportunities and approaches you have found to be successful for the purpose of developing the leadership potential of staff.

How do these compare with the accelerated leadership development opportunities listed above?

Which have had the greatest impact on your colleagues' development?

Consideration 5: How would we measure success?

Measuring the strategy's success

Having put in place your strategy for accelerating the leadership development of your staff, it is important for you to measure regularly and systematically how well you have achieved your objectives. Operating an ALD strategy can be expensive in terms of both time and money, and schools will need to be satisfied that their programme is cost-effective and provides value for money.

Possible measures

Despite the clear difficulties organisations face in trying to measure a return on their investment, several, for example Lilly UK, the National Audit Office and Corus, have each devised a series of metrics to help them assess the impact of their leadership development opportunities. Listed below are some possible measures of success, some of which will generate 'hard' data and others 'softer' data, such as perceptions or opinions. Both will be valuable in monitoring the progress of the strategy. Clearly, schools will want to tailor their measurements to their particular needs and systems. They might include:

- retention levels of staff exhibiting high potential;
- long-term performance of those deemed to be high-potential staff;
- percentage of those nominated as high-potential who progress to leadership positions within the expected time-frame;
- growth rate of the school's high-potential staff;
- extent and nature of the advancement of high-potential staff;
- frequency with which senior positions are filled by those who are not regarded as high-potential staff;
- frequency with which senior positions are filled from outside the school;
- high-potential staff's average time in post;
- the length of time leadership positions are open before being filled;
- quality of high-potential staff as measured by job performance problems, performance ratings, etc.;
- diversity of high-potential staff as measured by gender, race, etc.;
- reaction of high-potential staff to the school's strategy for acceleration;
- reaction of line managers to the attitude, performance and application of high-potential staff;
- reaction of headteacher/principal to the attitude, performance and application of high-potential staff;
- reaction of mentors to the attitude, performance and application of staff showing high potential.

The National College has developed Kirkpatrick's familiar model of evaluating training and ascertaining return on investment or impact (NCSL, 2008a: 83). The College proposes six levels of impact of development:

1. Reach – how many people take part in the development opportunities;
2. Engagement – participants say they enjoyed and valued it, captured through feedback forms at the end of the session or activity;
3. Learning – participants gain new knowledge and insights from the development, captured through assessments, tests and interviews;
4. Application – participants act differently in their daily role as a result of the development, captured through observation and feedback;
5. Impact on the school – participants contribute to improved organisational outcomes as a result of the development, captured through performance management and appraisal procedures;
6. Impact beyond the school – participants make a difference through consultancy, advice, mentoring or coaching in other schools.

Impact becomes more valuable but harder to ascertain as you go down the list. Matters are helped if you have some kind of baseline measurement so you know where you started from and how much progress has been made (Earley and Porritt, 2009).

> THINGS TO DO 6
>
> How do you know how effectively and efficiently your strategy accelerates the leadership development of your high-potential staff? What measures do you make use of to determine the impact of your strategy?
>
> With your impact measures in mind:
> What will you continue to do the same?
> What will you now do more of?
> What will you do less of?

Consideration 6: What risks do we need to consider?

Our final consideration concerns the element of risk. As with most initiatives, there is invariably an element of risk to consider. For example, with introducing an ALD strategy and system there are two key concerns around potential:

- Potential is not without risk – you can't guarantee that even the most talented leader will remain on any fast-track programme. For various reasons it may not work out as planned.
- Potential is not perfection – do not expect future leaders to possess every capability, to be fully rounded or have highly refined skills. We are looking for the seeds of senior leadership (adapted from NCSL, 2008a: 85).

The risks of succession planning are explored further in the final chapter with reference to Thomson's (2009) four risky assumptions.

Being aware of these concerns and potential risks increases the chances of the successful introduction of school-based ALD programmes. Schools will want to take into account the above six considerations in developing their strategy. They may also wish to conduct a leadership development survey to audit current practice and establish a baseline which will assist with the evaluation of impact.

Leadership development survey

As part of their wider work on leadership succession, the National College has produced helpful materials to assist schools and LAs with the succession planning process. The leadership development survey (see Figure 8.1) is a useful way of auditing current provision. Individuals are asked to assess how useful they would personally find the 15 leadership development activities listed and how effective they thought their school was at providing it.

Development activity	How useful would you personally find this activity?					How good is your school at providing this activity?				
	Not useful				Very useful	Very effective				Not effective
	1	2	3	4	5	1	2	3	4	5
Formal leadership programmes										
Coaching by leaders										
Mentoring										
Peer coaching										
Regular discussions										
Conferences and lectures										
Academic study/ qualifications										
Job shadowing										
Job rotation										
Temporary placements										
Leadership of special projects										
Performance management										
360-degree feedback										
Induction programmes										
Assessment centres										

Figure 8.1: Leadership development survey

(*Source*: NCSL, 2008b: 82)

Chapter 9

The challenge of fast tracking

- **The challenge of fast tracking**
- **The risks of succession planning**
- **The future of headship**
- **Final thoughts**

This chapter examines the consequences and implications of accelerated leadership development (ALD) programmes, talent identification and succession planning, and considers the risks and challenges they raise for schools and the wider education system. It also raises broader questions regarding the nature of senior leadership in schools and asks whether headship, as currently conceived, has a future.

The challenge of fast tracking

As has been shown throughout this book, there are significant challenges for fast-tracking leaders or implementing ALD programmes in schools and local authorities. Identifying talented staff and those displaying high potential is not an exact science and some argue that, like gifted and talented pupil programmes in schools, such early identification is not always helpful. A key question remains: how do such schemes fit in with schools', often stated, commitment to inclusion, diversity and equity? The business literature, however, suggests that we have neither the time nor the resources to develop all our people in equal measure and therefore we should concentrate on those who it is believed will benefit most.

There are already plenty of opportunities for career development in education so why, it might be asked, do we need to fast track individuals? Arguably, appointment panels (governing bodies) are rather traditional in their recruitment practices and are reluctant to appoint senior leaders who have not 'served their time' or acquired the necessary experience. It currently takes about 20 years to develop newly qualified teachers into headteachers – too long for some – and most schools in England have yet to develop cultures of talent development. However, the question of how individuals gain the necessary leadership experience is an important issue. Indeed, how can fast trackers gain experience rapidly other than by length of service? Leadership development schemes in some organisations involve moving jobs frequently, often with the individuals concerned not having to live with the consequences of their actions. Such fast trackers have sometimes been called 'mile wide, inch deep managers'. Similarly, we are all familiar with the phrase that 15 years' experience may simply be the equivalent of one year's experience repeated 15 times. If effective leadership of schools (and other organisations) is being able to draw upon the individual leader's stock of knowledge and experience to make what is felt to be the best decision at the time – what has recently been called *contextual intelligence* (Nye, 2008) – then how can people gain such experience rapidly?

Research by the Hay Group (2008) notes the difference between established leaders who show strengths in such matters as political awareness, indirect influencing, alliance-building skills and long-term thinking and planning, and emergent leaders and those on fast-track programmes who often do not. Of course, these qualities and skills are associated with experience and maturity, so how can leadership maturity be accelerated as well as leadership and management skills developed?

Nigel Collins makes the key point that people do not learn solely from experience: rather 'what we learn from is reflection on experience – and that needs time' (2008: 14). The key question, then, is how can opportunities for reflection be created? Schemes such as Future Leaders do try to create time and opportunities for reflection in a number of ways, but whether it is sufficient or not for successful headship is yet to be proven. However, evidence should be available soon because by 2009, 94 per cent of those who had completed the programme were in senior leadership team positions and four Future Leaders had been appointed headteachers, after only three years on the programme.

One of the main findings of the Teaching and Learning Research Project (TLRP) is that school teachers' and leaders' development is most effective when time is built into schools for reflection (James *et al.*, 2007). Opportunities to reflect with others (such as with a coach) can lead to even more powerful learning. Perhaps experience and maturity can to some extent be fast-tracked or accelerated given the existence of these factors to support it.

The risks of succession planning

Thomson (2009) has recently argued that there are four major risks inherent in most succession planning. These risks are important and are outlined below.

Risky assumption 1: Potential leaders can be identified

As has been shown, the literature largely assumes that leadership potential or talent can be recognised, but Thomson claims that there has been little debate about what constitutes talent and that there is an assumption that everyone will see the same things in the same people. She argues that talent identification is not straightforward and 'replete with all the contingencies and inequities attached to any judgement' (2009: 35). She asks: What counts as talent and how is it determined? Is there a tendency for people to select people just like themselves?

Thomson also points to the importance of context, stating that to show talent one must be in a situation where there is an opportunity to do so. 'So the question of talent spotting is as much about the school as an organisation and what affordances are offered to school staff to "be and become" leaders, as it is about what staff actually do' (2009: 36). She goes on to state:

> The risks inherent in talent spotting are that a narrow group is recognised as being worthy of leadership development. This in turn (re)produces existing (gendered and raced) norms of leadership and alienates those who have not been chosen. Failure to be 'spotted' might lead some to the decision to leave the profession altogether. It is vital that the role that the school and its existing leadership/ management may have had in producing the behaviours that are seen to constitute 'talent' are not ignored .
>
> (Thomson, 2009: 36)

Risky assumption 2: Potential leaders will identify themselves

Many programmes ask for volunteers, or aspirations for career development are outcomes of processes like performance review or appraisal. Thomson notes that the risks of relying on people identifying themselves are that:

> only some people will see themselves in and/or able to do the job, and thus a significant number of potential leaders will be lost to the system. This in turn will perpetuate a particular kind of leader/ manager, one who is overtly careerist and/or in an advantaged social and family situation.
>
> (Thomson, 2009: 37)

Risky assumption 3: Succession programmes create a pool of school leaders

According to Thomson, there are three difficulties with the assumption that a pool of leaders is created by succession programmes: training and application are not the same thing (i.e. some people see training as helping in their decision to become a headteacher or not); the number of aspirant heads does not equal posts being filled due to the unattractiveness of some positions; and targeting training is problematic.

Risky assumption 4: The way to get heads for hard-to-staff schools is to 'grow your own'

As we have seen, some schools (a growing number in the inner city) have 'resolved their supply problem by "growing their own" leadership through local talent spotting and the development of local succession schemes' (Thomson, 2009: 39). For such schemes to be successful there must be locally supported school-based practices, such as allowing teachers to experience leadership positions and to 'act up', giving them time to reflect individually and with others, providing input on educational leadership theory, and providing opportunities for such things as shadowing, coaching and visits to other schools, and the opportunity for conversations with experienced school leaders.

However, the risks with such home-grown schemes include a preference for local leaders rather than outsiders (new blood), the possibility of recycling less desirable practices, and the possibility that problems may arise when teachers attempt to leave 'home'. Such teachers may not be seen as having sufficiently broad experience. Thomson concludes that the risks involved in home-grown activities include 'the potential for inequitable practice to evolve, for the erection of unintended barriers to incomers and for career stalling beyond the local environment' (2009: 40). Thomson also discusses the appeal of the top job and it is to the future of headship that we now turn.

The future of headship

At the beginning of this book, reference was made to the 'demographic time-bomb' and the future challenge to national education systems in England and elsewhere of filling headship vacancies. Howson's 2007 report to the headteacher associations on senior staff vacancies found that 35 per cent of primary, 19 per cent of secondary, and 33 per cent of special school headships remained unfilled after the initial advertisement for the post (Howson, 2007a). These figures have not changed much since then (see Howson, 2009). In his earlier report he noted that 'what was once a problem facing a small number of schools, mainly in the primary sector, is now one that can challenge almost any school, anywhere in the country' (2007: 56). The 2007 report also noted that a significant proportion of headship vacancies (31 per cent of primary and 40 per cent of secondary) were advertised because headteachers were retiring before the age of 60. Heads retiring early will be doing so for a number of reasons, but it is known that a number take early retirement because of ill-health (in 2007, 6 per cent of primary and 2 per cent of secondary heads). With the current shortage of applicants for headships – and Howson's 2007 survey noted that the average number for all heads was marginally higher in 2007 but lower for deputy head posts – can the system afford to 'lose' such large numbers of school leaders through voluntary early retirement?

It is partly for this reason that growing attention has been given not only to ALD but also to the retention of senior school leaders, with a greater focus on their welfare and wellbeing. Are heads leaving their posts because of ill-health caused by excessive workload and stress, or is it that the job has become less 'do-able' and that the satisfactions obtained earlier from 'the best job in education' are now missing? As John Dunford, the general secretary of one of the headteacher associations, noted, 'school leadership is a rewarding job but government micro-management and increasingly job vulnerability are discouraging good candidates from taking on these roles' (cited in Slade, 2007). Are heads leaving their posts early for similar reasons, or to take up the myriad opportunities now available to them as educational consultants, inspectors, etc., where they can earn equivalent salaries without the high-stakes accountability pressures and stress increasingly associated with headship (see Earley and Weindling, 2006)?

Why heads leave or remain in headship is an important but relatively unexplored area. The key question is why heads leave the job *before retirement,* and Bottery (2006) found that most love the job and would only consider early retirement if they saw themselves as no longer having an impact, were no longer effective, or if they were too ill to continue. Yet, as noted above, it is known nationally that up to 40 per cent of heads retire or leave headship before they have to. Wellbeing, welfare and workload – the three Ws – are crucial. The National College has undertaken research into the working life of headteachers with the aim of gaining a better understanding of the nature of the job, workload, work–life balance and wellbeing (Nightingale, 2007; NCSL, 2007b). The final report of the project, entitled *A Life in the Day of a Headteacher* (NCSL, 2009c), identifies some of the practices and strategies that heads use to help them survive the many demands made on them.

As Fidler and Atton (2004) have argued, the future of headship must be one where the job is seen as more attractive and more manageable than currently it is. They suggest that the following need consideration:

- better preparation before headship;
- reducing the demands of the job;
- support and development in the job;
- recognition of the limited length of effective headship.

As has been shown, the National College argues for the importance of local solutions to succession planning and is questioning the time it takes for a teacher to become a headteacher (typically 20 years as the average age of new secondary heads is 43, a figure that has not changed in over 25 years – see Earley and Weindling, 2004; Slade, 2007). The College also argues that the demographic challenge is compounded by negative perceptions of the work and role of school leaders. Their advice to ministers therefore included:

- the need for local solutions (in 2008, 12 'leadership succession' pilot projects ran in schools and local authorities to develop the pools of leadership talent);
- a campaign to 'talk up' headship (since the overwhelming majority of heads are very positive about their work);
- giving opportunities for existing school leaders to gain self-confidence to do the job of headship;
- more fast tracking for those with leadership potential (NCSL, 2007a).

In the future, greater consideration will also need to be given to new models of headship such as co-leadership, executive and federated heads (NCSL, 2009b; DfES/PwC, 2007; Higham *et al.,* 2009). Distributed leadership is also seen as helping to reduce the load on the chief executive at the top of the organisational apex. So demanding is the role of the head today that they must surround themselves with good people; a move is needed from an emphasis on the individual headteacher to one of inter-dependence. Distributed and shared leadership does not, however, prevent 'the buck' continuing to stop with the headteacher.

Final thoughts

The development of school leaders and future heads through fast-track leadership schemes is likely to continue. As noted in Chapter 7, the Future Leaders programme has scaled up to a total of over 150 participants, with three cohorts in London, one in Manchester (from 2008) and another in the Black Country from 2009. Also, as other innovative programmes such as 'Teach First' and 'London Challenge' spread to other urban centres in England the same is likely to happen with the Future Leaders and other ALD schemes. For example, the DCSF's 'Children's Plan' (DCSF, 2007) talks, inter alia, about the expansion of the Future Leaders programme and its extension to other City Challenge areas. We have also seen the recent introduction of the National College's Accelerate to Headship programme, which encompasses Future Leaders and the new Tomorrow's Heads programmes.

The new ALD programme has places for about 200 candidates each year and participants are expected to also gain NPQH and become heads within four years. Much of the training takes place in teachers' own schools and there is a 'stretch assignment' to prove they can work well in a different school or other kind of institution. To gain a place on this new ALD programme, candidates have to pass a rigorous assessment linked to the NPQH/headship standards, covering everything from their 'vision' to emotional intelligence. The assessment procedures are built around a framework of 13 competencies that are informed by the six National Standards for Headteachers and grouped around 'Being', 'Thinking' and 'Leading' (see Figure 9.1).

Being	Thinking	Leading
Self awareness	Analytical thinking	Impact and influence
Resilience and emotional maturity	Conceptual thinking	Inspiring others
Integrity	Curiosity and eagerness to learn	Holding to account
Personal drive		Relating to others
		Developing others
		Collaboration

Figure 9.1: Accelerate to Headship: Tomorrow's Heads: 13 competencies

Successful applicants are expected to come from middle or senior school leadership posts, or from outside teaching. It will be interesting to see how many places go to bursars and other senior school business managers or indeed those with no educational background.

However, the successful completers of fast-track and ALD programmes must be able to change the mindset of the gatekeepers on selection panels, especially school governors. Will governing bodies be prepared to take the 'risk' of selecting a senior leader or headteacher from a non-traditional background, or one who has experienced rapid promotion? Also, will there be a greater acceptance of different models of headship as well as different routes to the top job and different kinds of people filling them, such as those without QTS?

Headteachers of state schools in England no longer need QTS and there are a very small number of bursars and school business managers who possess NPQH, the qualification for headship. How long before the first one becomes a headteacher? Indeed, the PricewaterhouseCoopers' report on models of school leadership is probably best known for its suggestion that people other than teachers be permitted to take up headship posts (DfES/PwC, 2007). However, as Fink (2010) argues, will they be able to lead the learning?

Chapter 10

Conclusion

This book has investigated programmes, initiatives and approaches to accelerated leadership development in both the private and public sectors in an attempt to bring out their main features and characteristics. It has also examined the main attributes associated with fast trackers and provided illustrations of high-potential and talent management programmes in both sectors. The overall aims of the book were not only to analyse accelerated leadership development provision, but also to develop practical knowledge to support activity in talent identification and fast tracking and to provide practitioner guidance.

Chapter 8 introduced an audit toolkit which, in part, has since become part of the National College's 'Evidence into Practice Guides', a series of guides that share intelligence and insights into the leadership succession challenges facing schools. Parts of the audit toolkit have been subsumed within the guide on 'Identifying Talent'. The 'Evidence into Practice Guides' published in 2008 and 2009 can be downloaded from the College's website (www.nationalcollege.org.uk/tomorrowsleaderstoday/resource).

This book has argued that there appears to be a strategic imperative for organisations throughout the world to manage and develop staff who show high potential and talent. Changing demographic patterns mean that more people are approaching retirement than entering the workforce. Younger generations of workers are said to have a different perspective on what it means to be an employee and are quick to look elsewhere if their present organisation is not meeting their expectations. Organisations, including schools, are becoming more aware of the need to 'invest in people' if they are to recruit and retain their workforce and if they are to perform well and become 'outstanding' or world class. Individuals, regardless of whether they are identified as high potential or not, if given few opportunities to grow and develop will move on and may well be lost to the profession forever. Over the years, some schools have been seen as 'training grounds for heads' where heads have taken great pride in the number of staff they were able to 'train up' for headship. What is now required, however, is for all schools to adopt such an approach, become adult learning-centred and be concerned for the development and training of all their staff. As noted in Chapter 5, the National College (NCSL, 2006) refers to them as 'Greenhouse Schools'.

Most leadership development strategies (accelerated or otherwise) consist of a combination of training programmes, mentoring and coaching, job exchange/rotation and action learning/action-research projects (usually work-related). Elements of each are found in various combinations in all of the ALD programmes outlined in this book. We also know as a result of this study that to get the most from high-potential staff, such individuals need:

- feedback;
- a rigorous development plan;
- room to reflect upon and capture their learning;
- a role that allows them to be fulfilled.

Developmental assignments that stretch people, such as challenging job responsibilities and task-force membership, work placements (NCSL, 2009d) and work shadowing (Simkins *et al.*, 2009) have more impact than training experiences – is this sufficiently acknowledged in our own ALD efforts in schools and local authorities?

The factors above are equally true, of course, of all staff development, whether fast tracked or not. The National College's report *Greenhouse Schools* (2006) shows how school leaders actively encourage and secure future leadership capacity by identifying, nurturing and developing leadership potential. As shown in Chapter 5, it proposes a range of strategies for growing tomorrow's leaders. It is important to identify potential leaders at the recruitment and selection stage and to provide opportunities for their development. But the key questions are: Should such opportunities be offered to all or just to those identified as having the potential to be future leaders? Will such staff select themselves? If so, they may not be the strongest – but perhaps the most self-confident. Is this also a matter of equity or equal opportunities for all – a strongly held value in most education systems? However, we do know that non-selected staff tend not to feel resentful provided that the selected (fast trackers or future leaders) can 'prove their worth'. Indeed, as we noted in Chapter 7, having individuals identified as future leaders or fast-track teachers in schools can have the unintended effect of encouraging others to seek promotion as they see themselves as 'just as good as them'.

Traditionally, career development and planning in schools has not been strong and there is a need for greater attention to be given to the training and development of all staff, teachers and support staff. In those schools that take leadership development seriously, all potential leaders have a strong chance of being developed and not only those who are identified (or self-select) as having high potential. Of more importance perhaps is the need to encourage teachers to want to take up leadership positions, to make the post of headship more appealing and attractive, and to have something to aspire to.

Many of the public and private sector ALD schemes considered in this book are found in large organisations or are part of *national* systems, and so their transfer to smaller units such as schools may be problematic. Size and scale are clearly important issues. For example, how might it be possible to introduce such a scheme in a small school, and are ALD schemes therefore only feasible (or desirable) in larger units such as local authorities, consortia, collaboratives, clusters or federations of schools?

How might solutions be found for the 24,000 state schools in England who are encouraged, given delegated budgets, to see themselves, and act, as individual autonomous units? A fast-track programme for an individual school may not make such sense, especially in return on investment or value for money terms. However, that does not mean that examples cannot be found although they are usually part of a broader CPD or leadership development programme (see such examples in NCSL, 2009b, 2009d and Matthews, 2009). The costs of ALD programmes, like other forms of CPD, must be met from school budgets. Local solutions in collaboration with others (e.g. schools or external bodies) may be the best way forward as any school on its own, even a large secondary school, is unlikely to be able to provide or afford a viable fast-track or accelerated programme. Schools will need to plan strategically, both with other schools and, where appropriate, with local authorities, to allow this to happen. Examples of leadership development programmes in LAs that have been developed as part of the National College's Leadership Succession Planning initiative are found on the College's website (see also National College, 2010).

It is worth stating that the debate about ALD is noticeable for the absence of any rigorous cost-benefit or return on investment analysis. The Fast Track Teaching programme (Chapter 6) was expensive and this was one of the reasons for its demise. The costs involved in putting people through a fast-track programme might be better spent in other ways (e.g. helping all schools to become Greenhouse Schools or making 'leadership' a more attractive option) or perhaps more efforts should be put into considering the potential of overseas trained and graduate teachers as future leaders? For example, many of these individuals with recently acquired QTS already possess many of the qualities and competencies needed for school leadership. This was also true of some of those on the Fast Track Teaching scheme. Similarly, should those individuals from outside the education sector who already possess considerable leadership and management skills but who wish to re-train or start second careers as teachers be fast tracked into senior leadership positions? These are difficult questions and views will no doubt differ.

In conclusion, the issue of identifying talented individuals and giving them accelerated development (preferential treatment?) has to be seen in terms of opportunity costs and against a backdrop of the traditional appointment practices of most governing bodies. Efforts and resources may be better deployed in other ways to ensure that effective leadership opportunities are provided for *all* those who might wish to become school leaders of the future. It is often said that those who wish to secure career advancement or promotion can do so reasonably easily provided that they possess the requisite skills, the talent and the motivation to aspire to such posts, and, most importantly, that they work in learning-enriched and not learning-impoverished schools. Our challenge must be to ensure that all schools are learning enriched for both staff and pupils.

References

Adair, J. (2003) *The Inspirational Leader*. London: Kogan Page.

American Association of Colleges for Teacher Education (2001) *PK-12 Educational Leadership and Administration*. Washington, DC.

Attfield, R. (2007a) 'What has been the impact of a programme of consulting and influencing skill on Fast Track Teachers and why has it been effective?' Unpublished report for CfBT Education Trust.

Attfield, R. (2007b) 'To what extent are the approaches of NPQH and Fast Track Teaching complementary and can improvements be made in the light of an emerging national strategy for succession planning?' Unpublished report for CfBT Education Trust.

Attfield, R. and Jones, J.L. (2007a) *Flying High: Some leadership lessons from the Fast Track teaching programme*. Reading: CfBT Education Trust and NCSL.

Attfield, R. and Jones, J.L. (2007b) 'Gauging the impact of the Fast Track teaching programme on the leadership of participants'. Unpublished report for CfBT Education Trust.

Barnes, I. (2008) *Identify and Grow your own Leaders*. Nottingham: NCSL.

Blass, E. (2007) *Talent Management: Maximising talent for business performance*. London: Chartered Management Institute.

Bolam, R. (2003) 'Models of Leadership Development'. In Brundrett, M., Burton, N. and Smith, R. (eds) *Leadership in Education*. London: Sage.

Bolam, R., McMahon, A., Stoll, L., Thomas, S. and Wallace, M. (2005) *Creating and Sustaining Effective Professional Learning Communities*. Research brief, Nottingham: DfES.

Bolden, R. (2005) *What Is Leadership Development?* Exeter: University of Exeter Leadership Centre.

Bolden, R. (2007) 'Trends and perspectives in management and leadership development'. *Business Leadership Review*, 4 (2), 1–13, April. Original source of Table 5.1 was West, M. and Jackson, D. (2002), 'Developing School Leaders: A comparative study of school preparation programmes', paper presented at *AERA Annual Conference*, New Orleans, April.

Bottery, M. (2006) 'Leaders and contexts: comparing English and Hong Kong perceptions of educational challenges'. *International Studies in Educational Administration,* 36 (1), 56–71.

Bryman, A. (1992) *Charisma and Leadership in Organisations*. London: Sage.

Bubb, S. and Earley, P. (2007) *Leading and Managing Continuing Professional Development*. London: Paul Chapman.

Bubb, S. and Earley, P. (2010) *Helping Staff Develop in Schools*. London: Sage.

Burns, J.M. (1978) *Leadership*. New York: Harper and Row.

Bush, T. (2004) 'The National College for School Leadership: purpose, power and prospects'. *Educational Management, Administration and Leadership,* 32 (3), 243–9.

Bush, T. (2008) *Leadership and Management Development in Education*. London: Sage.

Bush, T. and Glover, D. (2003) *School Leadership: Concepts and evidence*. Nottingham: NCSL.

Bush, T. and Jackson, D. (2002) 'A preparation for school leadership: international perspectives'. *Educational Management and Administration*, 30 (4), 417–29.

Byham, W.C., Smith, A.B. and Paese, M.J. (2002) *Grow Your Own Leaders*. Financial Times Press.

Castagnoli, P. and Cook, N. (2004) *Growing Your Own Leaders: The impact of professional development on school improvement*. Full Practitioner Report, Nottingham: NCSL.

Centre for Organisational Research (2001) *High-impact Leadership Development*. Available on line at www.cfor.org.

Charan, R., Drotter, S. and Noel, J. (2001) *The Leadership Pipeline: How to build the leadership-powered company*. San Francisco: Jossey-Bass.

Chartered Institute of Personnel and Development (2006) *Talent Management: Understanding the dimensions*. London: CIPD.

Chartered Management Institute and Ashridge Consulting (2007) *Talent Management: Maximising talent for business performance*. London.

Churches, R. and West-Burnham, J. (2008) *Leading Learning through Relationships: The implications of neuro-linguistic programming for personalisation and the UK government children's agenda*. Research paper, Reading: CfBT Education Trust.

Collins, J. (2001) *Good to Great: Why some companies make the leap…and others don't*. London: Random House.

Collins, N. (2008) 'Learning from reflection'. *Times Educational Supplement*, 4 January, 14.

Craft, A. (2000) *Continuing Professional Development: A practical guide for teachers and schools,* 2nd edition. London: Open University.

Crawford, M. and Earley, P. (2010) 'Personalised leadership development? Lessons from the pilot NPQH in England'. *Educational Review* (forthcoming).

Creasy, J., Barnes, I., Smith, P. and West-Burnham, J. (2004) *Meeting the Challenge: Growing tomorrow's school leaders.* Nottingham, NCSL.

Darling-Hammond, L., LaPointe, M., Meyerson, D., Orr, M.T. and Cohen, C. (2007) *Preparing School Leaders for a Changing World: Lessons from exemplary leadership development programmes.* Stanford, CA: Stanford Educational Leadership Institute.

Darling-Hammond, L., Meyerson, D., LaPointe, M. and Orr, M. (2009) *Preparing Principals for a Changing World: Lessons from effective school leadership programs.* New York: John Wiley.

Davies, B. (ed.) (2009) *The Essentials of School Leadership,* 2nd edition. London: Sage.

Davis, S., Darling-Hammond, L., LaPointe, M. and Meyerson, D. (2005) *School Leadership Study: Developing Successful Principals.* Stanford, CA: Stanford Educational Leadership Institute.

Day, C., Sammons, P., Hopkins, D., Harris, A., Leithwood, K. *et al.* (2009) *The Impact of School Leadership on Pupil Outcomes.* Nottingham: DCSF/NCSL. Research Report Number DCSF-RR108.

Day, C., Sammons, P., Hopkins, D., Harris, A., Leithwood, K., Gu, Q. and Brown, E. (2010) *10 Strong Claims about Successful School Leadership.* Nottingham: National College.

Day, D.V. (2001) 'Leadership development: a review in context'. *Leadership Quarterly*, 11 (4), 581–613.

Day, D.V. and Halpin, S.M. (2001) *Leadership Development: A review of industry best practices.* Fort Leavenworth Research Unit.

DCSF (2007) *The Children's Plan: Building brighter futures.* Nottingham: DCSF.

DCSF (2008) *Being the Best for our Children: Releasing talent for teaching and learning.* Nottingham: DCSF.

DfEE (1998) *Teachers: Meeting the challenge of change.* Nottingham: DfEE.

DfES (2004) *School Workforce in England.* G4. Nottingham: DfES.

DfES (2005) *School Workforce in England.* G4. Nottingham: DfES.

DfES (2006) *School Workforce in England*. G4. Nottingham: DfES.

DfES/PwC (2007) *An Independent Study of School Leadership*. Nottingham: DfES.

Draper, J. and McMichael, P. (2003) 'The rocky road to headship'. *Australian Journal of Education*, 47 (2), 185–96.

Draycott, S. (2003) *High flyers*. Session at CIPD conference, October 2003, Harrogate, UK.

Earley, P. and Porritt, V. (eds) (2009) *Effective Practices in Continuing Professional Development: Lessons from schools,* London: Institute of Education and TDA.

Earley, P. and Weindling, D. (2004) *Understanding School Leadership.* London: Paul Chapman.

Earley, P. and Weindling, D. (2006) 'Consultant leaders: a new role for headteachers? *School Leadership and Management*, 26 (1), 37–53.

Earley, P., Evans, J., Gold, A., Collarbone, P. and Halpin, D. (2002) *Establishing the Current State of School Leadership in England*. London: DfES.

Earley, P., Weindling, D., Bubb, S., Evans, J. and Glen, M. (2008) *Evaluation of the Future Leaders Pilot Programme*. Nottingham: NCSL.

Elmore, R.F. (2000) *Building a New Structure for School Leadership*. Washington, DC: The Albert Shanker Institute.

Fidler, B. and Atton, T. (2004) *The Headship Game: The challenges of contemporary school leadership*. London: Routledge.

Field, H.S. and Harris, S.G. (1991) 'Participants' frustrations in fast-track development systems'. *Leadership and Organisation Development Journal*, 12 (4).

Fink, D. (2010) *The Succession Challenge: Building and sustaining leadership capacity through succession management*. London: Sage.

Fink, D. and Brayman, C. (2006) 'School leadership succession and the challenges of change'. *Educational Administration Quarterly*, 42 (1), 62–89.

Fleishman, E.A., Mumford, M.D., Zaccaro, S.J., Levin, K.Y., Korotkin, A.L. and Hein, M.B. (1991) 'Taxanomic efforts in the description of leader behaviour: a synthesis and functional interpretation'. *Leadership Quarterly*, 2 (4), 245–87.

Fletcher-Campbell, F. (2003) 'Promotion to middle management: some practitioners' perceptions'. *Educational Research*, 45(1), 1–15.

Fullan, M. (2008) *What's Worth Fighting for in the Principalship,* New York: Teachers College Press.

Galpin, M. and Skinner, J. (2004) 'Helping high flyers fly high: their motives and developmental preferences'. *Industrial and Commercial Training*, 36 (3), 113–16.

Gardner, J.W. (1990) *On Leadership*. New York: Free Press.

General Accounting Office (2003) *Human Capital: Insights for US Agencies from other countries' succession and management initiatives*. October. GAO-03-914.

Goleman, D., Boyatzis, R. and McKee, A. (2002) *The New Leaders*. London: Little, Brown.

Goodall, J., Day, C., Lindsay, G., Muijs, D. and Harris, A. (2005) *Evaluating the Impact of Continuing Professional Development*. Nottingham: DfES.

Gritzmacher, P. (1989) 'Strategic management of fast-track employees'. *National Productivity Review*, 8 (4).

Guskey, T. (2000) *Evaluating Professional Development*. Thousand Oaks: Corwin.

Hargreaves, A. and Fink, D. (2006) *Sustainable Leadership*. New York: Jossey Bass.

Harris, S.G. and Field, H.S. (1992) 'High-potential management development programmes'. *Journal of Management Development*, 11 (1).

Hartle, F. (2005) *Shaping up to the Future: A guide to roles, structures and career development in secondary schools*. Nottingham: NCSL.

Hartle, F. and Thomas, K. (2003) *Growing Tomorrow's Leaders*. Available online at www.ncsl.org.uk/researchpublications.

Hay Group (2008) *Rush to the Top – Accelerating the development of leaders in schools*. London: Hay Group.

Hayes, T. (2005) *Rising Stars and Sitting Tenants: A picture of deputy headship in one London borough and how some of its schools are preparing their deputies for headship*. Summary Practitioner Enquiry Report, Nottingham: NCSL.

Hewitt Associates (2003) 'CEOs lead the way in leadership development among companies in Asia Pacific – Hewitt study finds'. Press release.

Hickman, G.R. (ed.) (1998) *Leading Organisations: Perspectives for a new era*. Thousand Oaks, CA: Sage.

Higham, R., Hopkins, D. and Matthews, P. (2009) *System Leadership*, Maidenhead: Open University Press.

Hirsch, W. (2000) *Succession Planning Demystified*. Brighton: Institute for Employment Studies.

Hollander, E.P. (1992) 'Leadership, followership, self and others'. *Leadership Quarterly*, 3 (1), 43–54.

Hopkins, D., Harris, A. and Jackson, D. (1997) 'Understanding the school's capacity for development: Growth states and strategies'. *School Leadership and Management,* 17 (3), 401-11.

Howson, J. (2007a) *The State of the Labour Market for Senior Staff in Schools in England and Wales 2005–6.* 12th Annual Report. Oxford: Education Data Surveys.

Howson, J. (2007b) *Aspects of the Labour Market for Teachers.* Report for CfBT. Oxford: Education Data Surveys.

Howson, J. (2009) *The State of the Labour Market for Senior Staff in Schools in England and Wales 2005–6.* 15th Annual Report.

Hudson Report (2007) *High Potential Programs: Investing in Long Term Business Leadership,* April–June 2007. Part 2.

IPPR (2002) 'The future of the teaching profession'. *Management in Education,* 15 (3).

Jago, A.G. (1982) 'Leadership: perspectives in theory and research'. *Management Science,* 28, (3), 315–36.

James, M., McCormick, R., Marshall, B., Black, P., Carmichael, P., Drummond, M., Fox, A., Honour, L., MacBeath, J., Pedder, D., Procter, R., Swaffield, S., Swann, J., Conner, C., Frost, D., Southworth, G. and Wiliam, D. (2007) *Learning How to Learn: In classrooms, schools and network.* London: Routledge.

Jones, J.L. (2005) *Management Skills in Schools: A resource for school leaders.* London: Paul Chapman.

Jones, J.L. (2007) 'Measuring the impact of CPD on the leadership development of Fast Track teachers'. Unpublished report for CfBT Education Trust.

Jones, P. (2006) *Review and Evaluation of the Fast Track Teaching Programme: Interim Report.* Report presented to the DfES by Shire Professional Chartered Psychologist. DfES Research Report No. 726.

Jones, P. (2008) *Review and Evaluation of the Fast Track Teaching Programme.* Nottingham: NCSL.

Kovach, B.E. (1989) 'Successful derailment'. *Organisational Dynamics,* Autumn, 18 (2).

Kovach, B.E. and Leonard, R. (2003) *High Flyers.* Session at CIPD conference, October 2003. Harrogate, UK.

Leibman, M., Bruer, R. and Maki, B. (1996) 'Succession management: the next generation of succession planning'. *Human Resource Planning,* 19 (3), 16–29.

Leithwood, K., Day, C., Sammons, P., Harris, A. and Hopkins, D. (2006a) *What We Know About School Leadership.* Nottingham: NCSL.

Leithwood, K., Day, C., Sammons, P., Harris, A. and Hopkins, D. (2006b) *Successful School Leadership: What it is and how it influences pupil learning*. Nottingham: NCSL.

Levine, A. (2005) *Educating School Leaders*. New York: The Education School Project.

Lincolnshire, L. (2005) *How the top 20 companies grow great leaders*. Hewitt Associates.

Lubitsh, G. and Smith, I. (2007) 'Talent management: a strategic imperative'. *360° The Ashridge Journal*, Spring, 9.

Lumby, J., Harris, A., Morrison, M., Muijs, D., Sood, K. and Glover, D. (2004) *Leadership, Development and Diversity in the Learning and Skills Sector*. London: LSRC.

Mabey, C. and Ramirez, M. (2004) *Developing Managers: A European perspective*. London: Chartered Management Institute.

MacBeath, J., Gronn, P., Opfer, D., Lowden, K., Forde, C., Cowie, M. and O'Brien, J. (2009) *The Recruitment and Retention of Headteachers in Scotland*. Edinburgh: Education Analytical Services, Scottish Government.

McCall, M.W. (1998) *High Flyers: Developing the next generation of leaders*. Boston, MA: Harvard Business School Press. Material cited was originally published in McCall, M.W. (1998) 'Developmental experiences'. *People & Strategy (Journal of HRPS)*, 12(1). Reprinted with permission.

McCartney, C. and Garrow, V. (2006) *The Talent Management Journey*. Horsham: Roffey Park Institute.

Matthews, P. (2009) *How do School Leaders Successfully Lead Learning?* Nottingham: NCSL.

Michaels, E., Handfield-Jones, H. and Axelrod, B. (2001) *The War for Talent*. Cambridge, MA: Harvard Business School Press.

National Audit Office (2006) *Improving Poorly Performing Schools in England*. London: NAO.

National College (2010) *Working Together: How local authorities and dioceses are jointly supporting effective succession planning and leadership development in schools*. Nottingham: National College.

NCSL (2001) *A Framework for Leadership Development*. Nottingham: NCSL

NCSL (2006) *Greenhouse Schools: Lessons from schools that grow their own leaders*. Nottingham: NCSL

NCSL (2007a) *What We Know about School Leadership*. Nottingham: NCSL.

NCSL (2007b) *Leadership Succession: An overview*. Nottingham: NCSL.

NCSL (2007c) *What We Know about Succession Planning*. Nottingham: NCSL.

NCSL (2008a) *Review of the landscape: leadership and leadership development 2008*. Nottingham: NCSL.

NCSL (2008b) *Leadership Succession: A framework for action*. Nottingham: NCSL.

NCSL (2009a) *What are we learning about…identifying talent?* (Evidence in Practice Guide). Nottingham: NCSL.

NCSL (2009b) *School Leadership Today*. Nottingham: NCSL.

NCSL (2009c) *A Life in the Day of a Headteacher*. Nottingham: NCSL.

NCSL (2009d) *Growing New Leaders and Leadership Capacity through Placements*. Nottingham: NCSL.

NCSL (2009e) *What are we learning about…effective local solutions to support succession planning?* Nottingham: NCSL.

National Policy Board for Educational Administrators (2001) *Recognizing and Encouraging Exemplary Leadership in America's Schools: A proposal to establish a system of advanced certification for administrators*. Washington, DC.

Nightingale, J. (2007) 'Routes forward'. *LDR*, 25, January, 18–21.

Northouse, P.G. (2004) *Leadership: Theory and practice*. London: Sage.

Nye, J. (2008) *Contextual Intelligence*. Oxford: Oxford University Press.

O'Donoghue, T. and Clarke, S. (2010) *Leading Learning: Process, themes and issues in international contexts*. London: Routledge.

Oliver, K. and Vincent, R. (2000) 'Management development: what gets results?' *Selection and Development Review*, 16 (6), 14–15.

Peterson, K.D. (2002) 'The professional development of principals: innovations and opportunities'. *Educational Administration Quarterly*, 38 (2), 213–32.

Pont, B., Nusche, D. and Moorman, H. (2008) *Improving School Leadership: Policy and practice*. Paris: OECD.

Robinson, V.M.J., Lloyd, C.A. and Rowe, K.J. (2008) 'The impact of leadership on student outcomes: an analysis of the differential effects of leadership types'. *Educational Administration Quarterly*, 44, (5), 635–74.

Roffey Park (2004) *Building Global Leadership*. Roffey Park Institute.

Rost, J.C. (1990) *A Force for Change: How leadership differs from management*. New York: Free Press.

Sandler, S.F. (2002) 'The growing importance of leadership development'. *HR Focus*, 79 (11), 13–15.

Shaw, M. (2006) 'New signs of crisis in leadership recruitment'. *Times Educational Supplement,* 3 January, 2.

Simkins, T., Close, P. and Smith, R. (2009) 'Work shadowing as a process for facilitating leadership succession in primary schools', *School Leadership and Management*, 29, (3), 239–52.

Slade, B. (2007) 'Skyward reach of a young gun'. *Times Educational Supplement*, 17 August, 14.

Speck. M. and Knipe, C.O. (2005) *Why Can't We Get It Right? Designing High-Quality Professional Development for Standards-Based Schools*. California: Corwin Press.

Taylor, D. (2002) *The Naked Leader*. London: Capstone.

Taylor, M., De Guerre, D., Gavin, J. and Kass, R. (2002) 'Graduate leadership education for dynamic human systems'. *Management Learning,* 33 (3), 349–69.

Thomson, A., Mabey, C., Storey, J., Gray, C. and Iles, P. (2001) *Changing Patterns of Management Development*. Oxford: Blackwell.

Thomson, P. (2009) *School Leadership: Heads on the block*. London: Routledge.

Thomson, P., Blackmore, J., Sachs, J. and Tregenza, K. (2003) 'High stakes principalship – sleepless nights, heart attacks and sudden death accountabilities: Reading media representations of the United States principal shortage'. *Australian Journal of Education,* 47 (2), 118–32.

Tomlinson, H. and Holmes, G. (2001) 'Assessing leadership potential: Fast track to school leadership'. *Journal of Educational Administration*, 39 (2), 104–117.

Tulgan, B. (2001) *Winning the Talent Wars*. New York: Norton.

Weindling, D. and Earley, P. (1987) *Secondary Headship: The first years*. Windsor: NFER-Nelson.

West-Burnham, J. (2004) *Leadership and Personal Effectiveness*. Paper presented at a seminar, Royal Garden Hotel, November. Nottingham: NCSL.

West-Burnham, J. and Coates, M. (2005) *Personalising Learning: Transforming education for every child*. London: Network Continuum Education.

West-Burnham, J. and Ireson, G. (2005) *Leadership Development and Personal Effectiveness*. Nottingham: NCSL.

Whitmore, J. (2003) *Coaching for Performance*. London: Nicholas Brealey.

Abbey (company) 38, 81
Accelerate to Headship programme
    64, 74–5, 91–2
accelerated leadership development (ALD)
    4–7, 10, 14–22, 41, 75–83, 86, 91–6
    customisation of strategy for 76
    extent of programmes for 21–2
    measuring the success of 82–3
    methods of 34, 50, 75
    new programme for 57
    in schools 45–74, 84
acceleration pools 18–19
'acting up' 89
action learning sets 33
adult learning 47–50
American Greetings Corporation 39
appointment panels 86, 95–6
'apprenticeship' to school leadership 7
assessment and development centres 33
Atton, T. 90
Australia 21–2, 34, 39–40

Barnes, I. 76
baseline measurements 83–4
Bass, E. 16
behavioural assessment 64
Bolam, R. 2–3
Bolden, R. 2–3, 34
Bottery, M. 90
Bubb, S. xii, 47, 51, 58, 98, 100
Bush, T. 3–4
Byham, W.C. 18

capacity building in schools 45
career changers 56–7
career development 28, 94–5
Castagnoli, P. 50
Centre for Organisational Research 32, 48
Chartered Institute of Personnel
    and Development (CIPD) 15
Children's Plan 91
Churches, R. 58
coaching 56, 70–1
Collins, J. 10
Collins, N. 87
competency frameworks 25
contextual intelligence 87
continuing professional development (CPD)
    58, 60, 95
Cook, N. 50
Corus (company) 82

Darling-Hammond, L. 46–7
Davis, S. 7
Day, D.V. 2–3
Department for Children, Schools
    and Families (DCSF) 1, 65, 91
Department for Education and Skills 56
deputy heads 50
'derailment' of careers 25–7
development opportunities 28–9, 50
developmental experiences 31–2, 48–9, 93–4
distributed leadership 91
Draper, J. 50–1
Draycott, S. 23–4
Dunford, John 90

Earley, P. 2, 50
early retirement 89–90
electronic learning (e-learning) 34

fast-track leadership development 5,
    34, 42, 50, 54–64, 75–85, 91–6
    selection of participamts for 29–30
    characteristics of participants in 22–3
    challenges posed by 86–7
Fidler, B. 90
Field, H.S. 23
Fink, D. 6
Fletcher-Campbell, F. 50
Fujitsu 29, 77
Fullan, M. 10
Future Leaders programme 55, 64–74, 77,
    87, 91–2
    destinations of participants in 72
    phases of 66–72
    impact of 73–4

Galpin, M. 24, 33
Garrow, V. 9, 23
Goodall, J. 58
'greenhouse schools' 51–4, 94
Gritzmacher, P. 22
GROW model 60

Hargreaves, A. 6
Harris, S.G. 23
Hartle, F. 19
Hay Group 26, 54, 76, 87
Hayes, T. 50
headship
    future for 89–91
    perceptions of 6

recruitment to 5–8
    vacancies for 5, 89
health problems 89–90
'high flyers' 60
'high potentials' and 'high-potential'
    programmes 19, 22–3, 38–41
Hirsch, W. 15
Honda 81
Howson, J. 5, 7, 63, 89
Hudson Report (2007) 21–2, 34

interpersonal and intra-personal skills 68

Jones, J.L. 60
Jones, P. 61–4

Knipe, C.O. 47
Kovach, B.E. 23–5

leader development 3
leadership development 45–8, 54, 60, 87
    concept and definition of 2–4
    content of programmes for 45–7
    as distinct from leader development 3
    as distinct from management 3
    high-impact systems for 48
    key trends in programmes for 46
    methods of 31–4, 37–8
    on-the-job 34
    structure for 58
    see also accelerated leader-
    ship development; fast-track
    leadership development
leadership development surveys 84–5
leadership effectiveness 64
leadership learning, personalised
    approach to 58–60
leadership of schools 64
    stages in 47
'leadership pipeline' model 19
leadership potential 2, 5, 9, 22–6, 50–4,
    75, 84, 88, 94
    early warning signs of 76
    personal characteristics
    associated with 22–5
    see also 'high potentials' and
    'high-potential' programmes
Leibman, M. 15
Leithwood, K. 64
Leonard, R. 24–5
Lilly UK 38, 82
Lloyds TSB 30, 38

local education authority (LEA) advisers 50
Lubitsch, G. 17
Lumby, J. 4
Mabey, C. 33–4
MacBeath, J. 6, 51
McCall, M.W. 24–5, 31–2, 48–9, 60
McCartney, C. 9, 23
McMichael, P. 50–1
managers' role in leadership
    development 25–6, 28
mentoring 48, 70
Minnesota Department of
    Transportation 38–9

National Audit Office 1, 82
National College for Leadership of
    Schools and Children's Services
    (formerly National College for School
    Leadership) 4–6, 9–10, 15, 26, 30,
    44–7, 50–5, 61–6, 74–5, 83–4, 90–4
National Health Service 81
National Professional Qualification for
    Headship (NPQH) 55–60, 63–4, 91–2
New Leaders for New Schools (NLNS)
    programme 65–6, 69, 74
New Zealand State Services Commission 39
Northouse, P.G. 1–2, 56

Oliver, K. 32

pay of teachers 61
Pepsico (company) 77
performance management systems 37
personalised learning 58–60
Police Service in Scotland 40–1

qualified teacher status (QTS) 66, 92, 95
quality of applicants for
    headship positions 7–8

Ramirez, M. 33–4
reflection on experience 87
retention of school leaders 56, 90
retirement of school leaders 6;
    see also early retirement
RHR International 25
risks
    of accelerated development 84
    of succession planning 87–9
Roffey Park Institute 33
Rolls Royce (company) 77
Royal & Sun Alliance 29, 38

Sandler, S.F. 49
Scotland 6, 40–1, 50–1
selection criteria for fast-track
    development 79
self-identification of potential leaders 88, 94
self-management of career
    development 28, 37
Skinner, J. 24, 33–4
Smith, I. 17
Speck, M. 47
sponsorship of staff with
    leadership potential 50
succession planning 8–10,
    15–16, 50–1, 54, 84, 90
    definition of 15
    as distinct from talent management 16
    risks of 87–9
Surrey County Council 81

talent
    definition of 35
    personal characteristics associated with 80
talent development 10, 36–7, 87
talent management (TM) 8, 15–21, 32, 58
    characteristics of schemes for 35–7
    definitions of 15–16, 19
    as distinct from succession planning 16
    operational impact of 21
    strategic perspectives on 16–20
talent spotting 50, 88 –9
Taylor, M. 45–6
Teaching and Learning Research
    Project (TLRP) 87
Thomas, K. 19
Thomson, A. 49
Thomson, P. 7, 87–9
3M (company) 77
Tomorow's Heads programme 74, 91–2
Training and Development
    Agency for Schools 51

United States 7–8, 38–9, 65, 69, 74

Vincent, R. 32

Weindling, D. 2
West-Burnham, J. 58
Western Australian Department of
    Resources Development 39–40
wider school focus 60